THE LOW ROAD

THE LOW ROAD

Walking the Walk for Veterans

*Thank you ♡
for helping our
heroes!*

Tommy Zurhellen

USN

Epigraph Books
Rhinebeck, New York

The Low Road: Walking the Walk for Veterans © 2021 by
Tommy Zurhellen

ISBN 978-1-954744-04-2

Book design by Colin Rolfe

Epigraph Books
22 East Market Street, Suite 304
Rhinebeck, NY 12752
(845) 876-4861
epigraphps.com

Tell me, O Muse, of that crafty veteran who traveled far and wide!
Many cities did he visit ... and much did he suffer
while trying to save his own life
and bring his brothers safely home.

—The Odyssey

For the
22 every day and the
40,000 every night

AUTHOR'S NOTE

To write this story, I depended on my personal journal, social media posts, selfies and videos, newspaper articles, follow-up conversations, research, and my own memory to recreate the events of my walk across America. Some names have been changed, and some have remained the same. Some identifying descriptions of people, places or events have occasionally been omitted, composited or altered to protect anonymity. You are encouraged to explore the "After/Words" section of this book, where I have invited the people who appear in this story to provide their own recollections and memories, in their own words.

Prologue

WARNING SIGNS

APRIL 15, 2020

I GUESS this whole thing started with a panic attack. A real doozy. This was a couple of years ago on the last day of the spring semester at Marist College, where I've taught the same writing classes for the last sixteen years. Looking back, I had been in a rut for a long time -- but when you're a tenured professor, damn, it sure is a comfortable rut. I remember being in a really good mood that day, giddy even, since I was about to embark on a whole-year sabbatical to work on another novel, my fourth. I can remember sitting in my cozy chair in my cozy little office, listening to Pandora on my desktop, waiting for my last few students to drop off final drafts of their stories and poems. Oddly I remember getting annoyed because somehow, a Coldplay song had just seeped into my Pandora queue -- when all of a sudden, *ka-zang*, it felt like a python twisting around my throat. I started sweating buckets. I couldn't breathe. I couldn't see, either; the room began to swirl like a Tilt-a-Whirl, the walls of this ride blurring into dense white fog, sugary and bright, like snow or cotton candy. *Poppies. Sleep.* No, this wasn't a dream. I hadn't been drinking, either. It felt like I was floating, and then, thanks to the laws of gravity, I slowly oozed out of my chair down onto my knees, arms limp at my sides, my head leaning forward until it finally rested against the cool linoleum floor. It looked like I was listening to railroad tracks for a distant train. Honestly, I thought I was about to die.

I remember thinking, *please God, don't let my students see me like this.*

I also remember thinking, *please God, don't let the last words I hear in this life be written by fucking Coldplay.*

Listen, I'm not supposed to suffer from panic attacks. At least, that's what I thought at the time. Look at me: I'm six and a half feet tall, several porkchops over 300 lbs. and built kind of like a Klondike bar -- but hey, let's imagine a *sexy* Klondike bar. I'm a proud Navy veteran with all the tattoos, scars, chipped teeth, bad knees, bitter sarcasm and suppressed emotions to prove it. I got two early life lessons from my Dad: one, always carry cash. And two, never talk about your feelings. Since then, I've been engaged two-and-a-half times but I've never been married; the common complaint has always been, "He never talks about his feelings."

Nailed it. Thanks, Dad!

Ask my students: I don't do drama. The only time I ever felt like wetting my pants was back in fifth grade, when Sister Mary wouldn't let me go to the bathroom so I sat at my desk behind Missy Schellenberger and literally *wet my pants*. True story. (Sorry, Missy.) So, if anything was going to put this beefy burrito on his knees, the smart money was on a good old-fashioned heart attack, right? Hell, I'd even go with *bear attack* before panic attack even entered my vocabulary. Shark attack? I'm game. Zombie attack? Bring 'em on! Cute attack, sure! But a panic attack? This guy? Oh, hell no.

But, silly bravado aside – I should have seen it coming.

You see, just a few weeks before, the universe decided to toss a wrench into that cozy, boring professor life I had been enjoying for so long: I was elected Commander of my local Veterans of Foreign Wars (VFW) Post here in Poughkeepsie, New York. If that sounds like a distinguished honor, it's not; I got the job because no one else wanted it. I was in my office at Marist one Wednesday night grading papers when my buddy Mickey called from the bar at the VFW to break the bad news. Mickey had spent twenty years in the Army and then another twenty as head custodian of a local community college, so he was used to giving orders to new guys like me.

"Congratulations, kid. You're our next Commander. It's official." Most of the guys at the Post call me *kid* even though I'm over fifty years old – which pretty much tells you all you need to know about the VFW. On the bright side, at least they don't call me *tiger* or *sport*. At least, not to my face.

Like all great cowards, I stalled. I tried to say no to this dubious honor without saying no. "Tell you the truth, Mickey, I didn't know I was nominated. I didn't even know we had *elections*."

"Exactly. It was a landslide, kid. You got an honest face."

"I don't know," I said, still looking for loopholes. "I don't want to step on anyone's toes. I mean, do I even have the right qualifications for the job?"

There was a long pause; I figured either he couldn't hear my voice over the bar noise, or he just wasn't paying much attention. Or both. I could hear some of the other guys talking in the background. "Exactly," Mickey said after a while. "Look, the last Commander stole fifty grand out of the Bell Jar, so we figured you couldn't do much worse. We've got confidence in you, kid." Somehow, I wasn't feeling the confidence. I barely knew these guys' names and they wanted me to be their fearless leader. "You being a college professor, too, we figured you probably know all about accounts and numbers and stuff."

"I teach English."

"Exactly," Mickey said. Then he hung up.

And that was it. I ordered my funny hat from the VFW online store and cleaned out a dusty storeroom at the Post for a makeshift Commander's office. Honestly, I didn't know much about the

VFW, even though I was a member. Growing up in the Bronx, it was just the place where old guys drank. But it turns out the VFW is the nation's oldest and largest service organization of combat veterans, with about 1.2 million members and thousands of Posts across the country. That's what it says in the brochure, anyway. I was surprised to learn not every vet can join the VFW; only those who served overseas in a theatre of conflict can be a member. In other words, the hard cases. So I decided to take the job seriously, which of course was my first mistake. I started off by waltzing into the offices of a few Poughkeepsie nonprofits that also help veterans, introducing myself as (drum roll, please) the new Commander at VFW Post 170. Please, please – no autographs at this time. Don't everyone genuflect at once.

"The VFW?" the first guy said, scratching his head. His name was Randy. "I didn't know we had one around here. Where is it?"

"Right down the street," I sighed, pointing out the window of his office.

"Oh," Randy said. "Sorry."

I was surprised just how competitive these nonprofits were with one another. Being the naïve new kid on the block with a funny hat, I just assumed we all worked together, since we shared the same goal of helping our local veterans, right? Wrong. It turns out that when you're competing for the same government grants and private donations, well, let's just say things can get pretty cruel in the business of kindness. I got a crash course, for sure. Harry Truman once said, "There's no limit to what we can do, when no one cares who gets the credit," but I'm guessing Harry never visited Poughkeepsie. Since I was still lucky enough to be flying under their radar, I didn't have to worry about throwing elbows in the whole roller derby/cage match they had going on between the established nonprofits in town. Capulets and Montagues, with me in the middle. I was surprised they left me alone.

At first, anyway.

I will say it wasn't all bad, meeting these folks at local nonprofits for the first time. At Hudson River Housing I met Christa, their Executive Director, and she was really the only person who welcomed my new energy in helping local veterans. We started cooking up ideas the minute I walked into her office in Poughkeepsie to introduce myself, and I have to admit, that was a pleasant surprise.

And I was in for plenty more surprises. We got a lot done in those first few weeks at the VFW, beginner's luck I guess: we set up a monthly picnic at our outdoor Pavilion for local homeless folks which fed around 100 hungry folks per night, and we started a new backpack program that donates 500 bags full of essentials like toiletries, socks and portable food to local folks in need each year. Our VFW Post also landed partnerships with both Bombas and Heat Holders, so we can distribute thousands of pairs of socks in to those in need, every year.

It was right around that time when I got my first call. It was actually a message on my cell from a guy named Freddy, who works with Christa at Hudson River Housing as their veteran program coordinator. "I hear you're the big guy at the VFW helping vets," his message said. "Well, I've got one for you. Call me back."

When I called Freddy back, he told me about a local Navy vet in need: single mom with five kids, aged from 15 to 5, and the two youngest had special needs. She was holding onto a full-time job but suffered from severe PTSD from her service in the Navy, and was on 100% disability. "Long story short, her broke-ass car finally broke," Freddy told me over the phone. "For good. We found her a minivan, and the dealer is willing work with her, but she doesn't have money for a down payment." He drew a long breath of desperation; I could tell I was probably the tenth or twentieth person he had reached out to on this veteran's behalf. "Do you think the VFW could help?"

Other members at the VFW balked when I told them the story. One shrugged his shoulders and said, "Sounds like a job for social services." But I didn't care. I saw it differently: this was a fellow veteran who needed help, and needed it now. So I called the dealer that day, worked out a deal for the down payment, and walked a check over the next morning. I felt so much satisfaction, knowing I did something to make someone else's life better. When was the last time I felt an amazing rush like that?

Honestly, maybe never.

Freddy called me a few days later to follow up and say thanks. "She can't thank you enough. She's driving her kids to the doctor as we speak." Then he laughed out loud. "You better get some rest, big guy."

"Why's that?"

"When the word gets out, you're going to get a lot more calls. There's lots of vets around here who need help, but a lot of them fall through the cracks."

It turned out Freddy was completely right. I started fielding about a call a day from either local vets or nonprofits seeking help for a vet: money problems, transportation problems, health problems, problem problems. I got frustrated very quickly, simply because I couldn't help everyone. Our VFW had limited resources and I already had a full-time job. I was embarrassed; until that moment I had no idea how bad it was for so many veterans living right in my own community. And when I did some research, I realized it was bad all over America: according to a recent VA study, 22 veterans take their own lives every day in America. That's double the suicide rate for civilians; for female veterans, it's triple. And every night, over 40,000 of our veterans find themselves homeless every night, enough to fill Yankee Stadium.

Something had changed inside me, almost overnight. It was clear I'd found a true passion – or rather, that passion had found me. I had always assumed I was making a difference as a teacher, helping my students find their voice in their writing. As professors, we always tell our students to go out and change the world.

But when was the last time we went out there and tried to do it ourselves? I had opened a Pandora's Box of self-loathing and I had no idea how to shut it. Now whenever I sat in my Marist office, I would simmer in silence listening to my colleagues down the hall wax poetic about big, lofty ideas with their students, the same way I had always done for these past 16 years. I had "talked the talk" in the lofty heights of the Ivory Tower for so long, I had forgotten what it was like to walk the walk on common ground. Suddenly I felt like a complete pretender and hypocrite, sitting up there in my cozy office every day while there were so many other veterans struggling, right outside my window.

"You can't help everyone," Mickey told me one day at the VFW, over a beer.

"I know." But inside I was saying, *like hell I can't.*

I started having trouble sleeping. I would toss and turn most nights, wrestling with these fresh demons. Other nights I would stay up reading endless stacks of library books on subjects and causes I had no idea existed, like effective altruism and the "80,000 Hours" movement. I was surprised to find there were so many other people grappling with the same questions I had started asking myself. All these books seemed to be trying to answer the same question from different philosophical perspectives:

Can one person change the world?

Now I was locked into my own fool's errand, working seven days a week trying to help veterans in Poughkeepsie with the limited resources we had at the VFW. For all that effort, it still felt like taking a bucket out of the ocean. Until one night, when I woke in another hot sweat around three a.m. and went to the bathroom to splash some cold water on my neck. I ended up just standing there staring into the mirror at the tired, naked Klondike bar staring back. I'll admit I've always disliked looking in mirrors, thanks to a lifetime of being a fat kid with body issues, but hey, that's a different book. No, this was something different, something much bigger. This was disgust. This was shame. This was panic. *Just look at you*, I started to mutter at the mirror, over and over. *Just look at you making a difference out there, kid. Just look at you. Just look at you, changing the fucking world.*

I must have gotten pretty loud, because the next thing I know my fiancée at the time sprang into the doorway, clutching a George Foreman grill with both hands, ready to swing. She thought I'd cornered a burglar in the bathtub or something. But when she looked around and realized I was alone, the look in her eyes sank from beast mode into bewilderment.

"What the hell are you doing?" she said.

I was still staring hard at the loser in the mirror. "Nothing," I sighed. "Absolutely nothing."

We ended up having a good talk that morning over coffee, but I couldn't explain why I was yelling at myself in the mirror. (For the record, she couldn't explain what she planned to do with the George Foreman grill, so we called it a draw.) But as hard as I tried, I couldn't articulate exactly what I was feeling inside. I couldn't tell her why I suddenly felt so passionate about something I didn't even know existed a month ago. One thing was certain: I couldn't spend my upcoming sabbatical sitting around writing some silly novel. I had a fire burning inside to do something, but I couldn't explain what that something was. I couldn't even explain why my cozy life felt like it had been completely turned upside down.

I still can't.

You already know what comes next. Later that same day, I'd be down on my knees in my campus office, tortured by Coldplay, weighed down by the gravity of good intentions, falling on imaginary railroad tracks, waiting for my train to come.

They say the road to hell is paved with good intentions. Turns out they were only part right; if you're walking, you quickly find out the road ain't paved at all. Trust me on this one. When you walk that lonely road, along with your good intentions I guarantee you'll find plenty of loose gravel, soft shoulder, no shoulder, mud, muck, roadkill, mosquitoes, biting flies, more roadkill, sinkholes, potholes, puddles, puddles that turn out to be sinkholes when you step in them, even more roadkill, rattlesnakes, bull snakes and red anthills the size of sandcastles. You will find angry bees, angry dogs, angry truckers, angry truckers with angry dogs riding shotgun, angry signs that warn you to *keep out* or *keep off* or *keep moving* or *keep Jesus in your heart*. You will find chain gangs, motorcycle gangs, actual gang gangs, abandoned vehicles, abandoned gas stations, entire abandoned towns, roadside motels full-up and roadside churches burnt down. You will find closed sidewalks, crushed beer cans, construction vehicles, confused construction workers wondering what in hell you're doing on foot way out here in the middle of nowhere, confused state troopers and sheriffs wondering the same thing, old cigarette butts, old keys, used needles, used crack pipes, a used car seat with a stuffed animal strapped in, used condoms, half-eaten French fries mixed with more roadkill. You will find millions of cows, cow crossings, cow skulls, cow shit, horse shit, bear shit, all kinds of bird shit, unidentified shit, your own shit, leg cramps, diarrhea, dehydration, sunburn, twisted ankles and missing toenails. You will find out what *plantar fasciitis* means. You will find many wrong turns, several good Samaritans, bad directions, bad drivers, bad weather, broken glass, lost cattle, lost tourists, one lost tooth (it's in Nebraska) along with a few ghosts and plenty of wildflowers. And if you walk long enough, well, you just might find yourself.

So I'm going to propose a slight revamp on that age-old proverb. The road to hell is paved with good intentions, yes. But only if you're driving. If you choose to walk that unholy path to perdition, I'm here to tell you it's definitely *un*paved. With good intentions. And a lot of roadkill.

This is the story of a man trying to walk that walk. Exactly one year ago today, on a chilly April morning, I got dropped off at the city limits of Portland, Oregon with the modest goal of walking the 2,866 miles back home to Poughkeepsie, New York. No support vehicles. No marked trail. No media entourage (at least, not at the start.) Really all I had with me that first day was a mailbag, my VFW windbreaker, a phone, and my sense of humor. Even after several months of training and planning for this grand adventure, I was still woefully out of shape, and even more woefully unprepared.

What could possibly go wrong?

Well, everything, of course. And while it's true I had absolutely no idea what I was doing, that was kind of the point. Colin Powell once said, "Don't step on enthusiasm." In other words, don't sweat the small stuff. Sometimes you go with what you've got. At some point, you realize you don't need a map because you *are* the map. Sometimes you have to let life write on you. You have to step out of your comfort zone. You have to take a risk.

That's the theory, anyway.

Right now, I'm sitting on my girlfriend's porch with my laptop and a cup of weird tea, trying to figure out how to write this book. Today is April 15, 2020, a whole year to the day after I started walking across America, and it's taken me this long to just to come up with a title. Every time I stare at this blank screen I feel like I'm getting further and further away from what I want to say. We're smack dab in the middle of the coronavirus pandemic here in New York, so with normal life shut down for an unessential worker like myself, there are zero excuses *not* to write. I learned so much every single day out there on the road: about veterans, about America, and most importantly, about myself. There's probably enough material in my head for three books, or at least a few seasons on Netflix. But I still have so many questions, and I'm starting to wonder which is going to be tougher: walking across the country alone, or writing about it?

Oops! I must be talking through these questions out loud, because my girlfriend just shouted at me out the window. "Write about peeing yourself, and running out of water!"

Okay, spoiler alert: at some point, the hero of this story is going to pee himself.

Also, he will run out of water. Not necessarily in that order.

If you're still reading this book, you probably have a lot of questions, too. Questions like, where *did* you go to the bathroom out there? What did you eat? Where did you sleep? What does sunrise in Wyoming look like? Did you keep that tooth you found on the side of the road? Does everyone in America hate each other? Did you make it home in one piece? And perhaps most importantly, is this book going to be like *Eat, Pray, Love*? Hey, I admire that book, too. We probably admire it for the same reasons: it's an uplifting journey of self-discovery. It's the kind of book that makes you look up at the clouds when you feel like you're stuck in the mud. It's a search for the high road in life.

Listen, this book is not going to be anything like *Eat, Pray, Love*.

We've always been told to take the high road. Ever since our first schoolyard fight when we came home with a bloody nose, our moms have universally said, *you should have taken the high road*. And when we got a little older and mom saw us passing a joint with other kids in the same schoolyard, she said something like, *and if they jumped off the Empire State building, would you jump too?* In other words, don't stoop to their level, kid. I didn't raise you to get dragged down into the gutter. Whenever they go low, you go high. Always rise above. Always turn the other cheek. Always take the high road.

Thanks, Mom!

Over the years, that lofty advice has certainly served us well. It's basically become our gospel when dealing with others – especially now in this weird age of social distancing. It helps us avoid conflict. When someone tells us to take the high road, they're basically warning us to take a step back, to disengage. But I think we often forget the high road is really the freeway, the convenient way, the easy way. When we choose the high road, we want to get to wherever you're going as quickly as possible. It's all about the destination, not the journey. Too often we choose the express lanes in life, automatically bypassing the problems affecting other people, problems often way more serious than our own. When we only walk the high road, we develop empathy problems. We forget how to understand the lives of others, even when they live right next door. We get lazy. The way I see it, we can only learn so much about our world up there on the freeway, whizzing by with our windows up while so many people down below deal with issues we have no clue how to even talk about.

So here's my theory: if you really want to change the world, you have to learn how to take the low road. You have to get your hands dirty. You have to engage. You have to look folks straight in the eye, on the same level, not by looking down. You have to listen up close. Sure, the low road is going to be rougher and slower, but isn't that the point? At least it won't be boring. When you commit to the low road, the destination really doesn't matter. It's all about the journey, the *now*, the road less traveled we can see winding its way, just ahead. Sometimes you have to take a wrong turn for all the right reasons. Sometimes you have to get low.

That's why this book is named *The Low Road*. I wanted to know what it truly feels like to be a homeless veteran in America today. I didn't want to read it in a book. I wanted to walk a few thousand miles in the shoes of thousands of women and men who are in crisis, to experience the real struggles in their lives; I also wanted to see just how much I've taken for granted in mine. I wanted to talk with veterans I'd never meet unless I actually walked right through their towns and neighborhoods. I wanted to listen to their stories and find out what they really care about, with no filter. I wanted to explore parts of our world we never see as we whiz by in traffic at eighty miles an hour.

But most of all, I wanted to find an answer to that question that had been consuming me ever since this whole rodeo started.

Can one person change the world?

Hey, if you're *still* reading this book, I'm guessing you've been asking yourself the same question lately. And I'm guessing you're wrestling with some similar demons. In that case, I'm really glad you're here. After all, nobody wants to face those demons alone. I really hope you stick with this book. I hope you use it to fuel your own foolhardy ideas to make the world a better place, because let's face it, we need more foolhardy ideas. If you've suddenly realized you have a passion for something, but you're not quite sure what to do about it, you are definitely in the right place. That was me, one year ago. There are so many worthy causes out there that need your raw energy, enthusiasm and strong voice, from #BlackLivesMatter and the #MeToo movement to fighting for LGBTQ equality and preserving the environment for future generations. At this very moment, there are women and men out there valiantly fighting the good fight to save children, defend immigrants, rescue animals, support artists – the list of important issues is almost endless. Whatever your passion, I hope this book helps you realize you don't need fancy advice, or fancy equipment, or a fancy degree to make a difference. You just need *you*. And maybe a sense of humor.

This isn't a self-help book. You won't find handy-dandy top ten lists of ways to change your chakras, and you won't find any philosophical lectures or sage advice lurking in here, either. You're just going to find a big guy in a funny hat trying to walk the walk, one day at a time. Besides, I'm pretty sure the only sage advice needed to kickstart any quest comes from that great American scholar (and WWII veteran) Yogi Berra: When you come to a fork in the road, *take it*.

See? You got this. Trust me on this one. After all, if this goofy Klondike bar can get off his butt and find the low road, you can, too. The spiritual teacher Ram Dass once said, "We're all just walking each other home." I hope you'll walk home with me, by reading this book.

Can one person change the world?

Well, I guess we're about to find out. Together.

Day 2

RHODODENDRON, OREGON

T HEY SAY a journey of a thousand miles begins with a single step. I believe the Chinese philosopher Lao Tzu said it first, about seven thousand years ago, and I said it myself just yesterday as I took my ceremonious first steps in Portland, to start this walk. I believe I'd still be saying it today, on Day 2, if my whole body wasn't engulfed in so much godawful, gut-wrenching, paralyzing pain. Look, I don't know how much actual walking old Lao Tzu did back in the day before he came up with that particular bit of wisdom, but I think he left out some parts. Like, *intentionally*. Sure, the journey begins with a single step, but it also begins with horrifying blisters between your toes, frightening new smells coming from your crotch and armpits, and terrifying chafing in regions of your body where you never imagined chafing. It begins with tossing your bloody socks into a motel garbage can and sticking your raw, scabby feet into tubs of ice just to get the swelling down.

The journey really begins with waking up on Day 2, unable to move your legs.

My alarm goes off at 6am but I'm already wide awake. I've been lying on my back in this lumpy bed for hours now, staring up at the stucco ceiling of this Best Western and thinking about a guy named

Edward Payson Weston. I've got plenty of time to daydream: I wasn't joking when I said I can't move my legs. I can't even bend my knees without whimpering in pain. My feet are numb, and even my eyebrows hurt; I'd rub them but my shoulders are so sore I can't lift my arm up to my head. It's still dark outside but the sodium lights in the motel parking lot are making the stucco ceiling look like an old photograph of the moon. I'm still wearing my clothes from yesterday, everything crusted with the same layers of salt and sweat. The alarm on my phone goes off again, but I still haven't moved to turn it off; it's supposed to be church bells but it sure feels like a funeral gong right now. *Ding dong. Ding dong.* My phone is only a few feet away on the nightstand, but it might as well be ringing on Mars, because I can't reach it.

Ding dong. Ding dong.

I start to cry softly. (Okay, it's more of a pathetic blubbering, like a lonely whale – but hey, this is my book.) It's true my body is in a lot of pain, but that's not really the reason I'm crying. No, I am crying because last night, after finishing my first 22 miles, I drank about thirty gallons of water (and a little whiskey) to recover and now, I have to go to the bathroom really, really, really, bad. And it's all I can do to prevent this queen bed from suddenly becoming the largest man-made lake in Oregon. Up in heaven, there's a nun named Sister Mary looking down at me, laughing her ass off and screaming *karma is a bitch, kid.*

Maybe I should just call out for help. The walls seem thin. I think my pain threshold has lowered enough to roll on my side, reach the room phone, and somehow hit zero with my forehead. I wonder if the desk manager has dealt with situations like this before. *Okay people, listen up! This is what we train for. We need a forklift, a roll of plastic sheeting, hazmat suits, and a whole lot of extra hand towels sent to Room 108, stat! Execute Plan Bravo. Let's move!*

I'm pretty sure my man Edward Payson Weston dealt with this, a long time ago.

One of the many books I read while planning this walk was a biography on the first recorded human to walk across America, in 1907. His name was Edward Payson Weston, and he was definitely a character; I guess he had to be since he was 70 years old when he set off from the steps of City Hall in New York City and headed for San Francisco. Thousands of people in cities and towns all across America came out to cheer him along, and just about everyone who saw him wondered how this old bird kept such a spring in his step and a smile on his face when he passed through their town. But my favorite part of that book about Weston is an account from a bellhop at a fancy hotel where Weston was staying when he reached Chicago. The bellhop said he was working the early morning shift. It was still dark out when he heard a terrible moaning coming from a back stairway; there were no elevators in this hotel yet in 1907. When the bellhop rushed to investigate, he saw Weston struggling to get down the stairs, one at a time, standing sideways with both hands on the rail, and cursing like a sailor the whole time. The bellhop estimated it took the old man a good half-hour just to get down that one stairwell. When Weston finally reached the bottom, Weston's face instantly returned to that trademark smile and the old man walked briskly out the lobby door with his walking stick, on his way to San Francisco. That's my favorite story from the book because it reveals the part no one was supposed to see, the ugly part where this famous guy is in so much pain from walking the day before, he can't even bend his knees to get down a staircase. And right now, I'm pretty sure I know exactly how the guy felt. At least the Best Western had the foresight to put me on the first floor, mercifully. That doesn't get me any closer to the bathroom, though.

Okay, I'm desperate so I decide to make a break for it. I start rocking my body back and forth on the bed, hoping I can get some momentum to roll over on my side. From there I'm hoping I'll find a way to find the floor, grit my teeth, and crawl my way to the bathroom. Baby steps. But when I rock back and forth, I get too much momentum and instead of rolling onto my side I roll all the way off the bed entirely, doing a full bellyflop onto the carpet. That hurt. But hey, I'm halfway there; all I have to do now is get up on my hands and knees and crawl to the bathroom. The problem is my knees won't bend, not even a little bit. Baby steps. So Plan B is crawling on my belly, side to side like a crocodile or platypus. As I waddle, friction from the carpet quickly forces my pants down to my ankles – which leaves my junk exposed to the carpet. Now it feels like someone is taking sandpaper to my junk every time I move. Anyway. I finally make it to the smooth tile of the bathroom. Home free! But wait. As I lie flat on the floor with my head next to the toilet, I realize physics or geometry are definitely not in my favor here.

Desperate times call for desperate actions, people. I frantically inchworm my body over to the edge of the walk-in shower, heave-ho onto my side and finally, this beefy battleship lets go with a full salvo that paints the walls of the shower stall for a good two minutes. If I didn't keep the next room awake with all the previous crying and moaning, well, they're up now, because I'm making that thunderous yawp you only make when you're either engaging the enemy on the field of battle, or taking a really long piss.

I will remain here on my back between the toilet and the shower for a little while. Looking up at the ceiling, I imagine Edward Payson Weston is staring down from heaven, too. He's standing alongside Sister Mary, and they're both peering down at this sad man with his pants down in a Best Western bathroom, trying his very, wide-eyed best to change the world. At least old Edward isn't laughing at me. No, he's just shaking his head with a knowing smile that says:

Welcome to the low road, kid.

Yesterday started with a lot more hope, and a lot less blubbering. Of course, I hadn't walked my first 22 miles yet, so I really had no clue about what was in store; I think the word we're looking for is *naive.* Day One officially began at 5am, waking up on a futon in my old shipmate Paul's house in the Portland suburbs, with an excited smile plastered across my face. *This is it!* I thought to myself. *This is going to be great!* Bright-eyed and bushy-tailed, I called into the *Boris & Robyn Morning Show* back in Poughkeepsie to give my first weekly update on the walk, with the three-hour time difference. They had been kind enough to invite me into the studio a couple months ago to announce the walk, my first media splash. When I walked into the studio back then, the first thing Boris said was, "You don't look like a guy who can walk across the country." He was right, of course. I remember Robyn was more hopeful at the time. I think when Boris said that, though, it gave me a little more determination. I've been a fat kid my whole life, even when I was a skinny kid, and I've gotten used to adding that grist to my mill.

"How are you feeling?" Boris asked when we went on air that morning on Day One.

"Great, I'm excited. I'm in Portland, ready to go," I whispered into my phone, trying not wake up Paul and his family this early. "The only bad thing is my walking stick got lost in the mail." Yes, I had sent it here by Fed Ex and the box actually showed up on Paul's porch the day before – but mysteriously the box was empty, with a big hole in one end. "So you know, I'll just have to start the walk without it."

"Bad omen," Robyn said. "Turn back."

"He hasn't started walking yet, Robyn," Boris said. "He's got to walk before he can turn back."

"Turn back anyway," Robyn said, her voice now fraught with worry, like a mom waving goodbye to her kid leaving for boot-camp. "Tom, are you sure you want to do this?" I'm not sure what I said in reply, but looking back, maybe I should have taken Robyn's warning to heart.

Everything went more or less to plan on the first day – except for the Curious Case of the Missing Walking Stick, of course. After breakfast, Paul and I got a ride from his wife out to the city limits where the Springwater Corridor Trail began. From there, we walked the first ten miles on the flat rail trail to its end, and then the last twelve miles were alongside Highway 26 until it reached the little town of Sandy. We were lucky enough to cross paths with three or four veterans along the trail; they were all Vietnam vets, and they all had the same, glassy-eyed stare of surprise when they learned I'm planning on walking across the country. In running shoes. And a windbreaker. And a mailbag.

"How far you get, so far?" one of the vets asked.

"It's his first day," Paul said cheerfully. "He's only got 2,800 miles to go."

We took a break after the first ten miles to rest and eat some lunch. My feet felt pretty good, but it might have been the adrenaline of the first day kicking in. Paul runs half-marathons, so I spent the day basically trying to keep up with his pace, which was too fast for a guy like me. But the miles went by fast as we talked about old times and updated each other on everything since we were still in the Navy, twenty-two years ago. I started to hit the wall around mile 15 or so, but luckily, Paul paced me the last few miles, and we finally made it into the town of Sandy just as a rainstorm was coming in. I checked into my room at the Best Western, stowed my gear, and we found a sports bar nearby to take a load off and have a few drinks. Paul had arranged to have his buddy drive out from Portland and pick him up that night, so we spent a couple more hours toasting to our success before his ride showed up.

"You did it," Paul said, lifting his Jack and Coke to clink mine. "Proud of you, brother. Day One down, and only like, two thousand more to go."

"A hundred and thirty-one," I said. "But who's counting."

I waited for Paul and his buddy to drive away before I stood up from my chair at the bar, to find the bathroom. I waited that long because, secretly, my feet hurt so much after walking 22 miles that I wasn't sure if I could stand up at all. I didn't want Paul to worry, or call an ambulance. When I sat down at the bar a couple hours ago, everything felt pretty normal. But now, everything has swelled up like my body was suddenly made out of balloons. A good night's sleep and a hot shower should knock everything back into place, though. Right?

Thankfully, Day Two of this outrageous adventure will end up the exact opposite of Day One: it will finish in a much better place than where it started. Today it's only a fifteen-mile hike to the next town along winding Highway 26; it's a little hamlet called Rhododendron where there's a guy named Mark tending bar at the VFW who's allegedly willing to let me crash in his spare bedroom for the night. And when I reach that VFW tonight after a sloppy, rainy day dodging big rigs along this busy mountain highway, it's mostly empty inside, save for a veteran sitting at the bar who is the spitting image of a silver-haired Burt Reynolds. Burt and I take turns buying each other rounds of Rainier beer from the tap and telling each other stories. Sitting at the bar, my feet are painfully swollen again like this morning, but at least they're recovering more quickly; tonight I can walk to the bathroom when I want, without crawling. Baby steps.

"How much further you got on this walk thing?" Burt Reynolds asks.

"Thirty-seven miles down," I say, doing the math. "Only 2,800 left to go."

"Forgive me for saying this," he says after taking a big breath. "But you don't look like a guy who's going to walk across the country."

"Yeah, I get that," I say with a smile. "A lot."

He nods before ordering us another round. "So why are you doing it?"

"Honestly, I don't know," I say. "Trying to raise awareness, I guess."

"Uh *huh*," Burt says as he looks around the empty bar. "And how's that going?"

Day 3

~~CLEAR LAKE CAMPGROUND,~~ OREGON

M Y PHONE rings around 5am, an hour before my alarm is
supposed to go off. I don't recognize the number, but it's
got an 845 area code so I know it's from back home in the Hudson
Valley. Three time zones away. I'm woozy from exhaustion and
a Rainier hangover so I shouldn't pick up, but my morning haze
makes me half-believe it could be an emergency, coming from
Poughkeepsie at an ungodly hour. Who knows, maybe it's my Dad
calling to say Mom is in the hospital. Or maybe its Mickey from the
VFW calling to say my pickup truck was stolen. Or maybe it's the
Fiancée, calling to confess she stole my pickup truck and pushed it
into a lake. Okay, I have an active imagination. Too active.

"Hello," I mumble into the phone.

"Hey hey, Tommy! How are you, my man?" The voice is cheery.
"It's Randy."

"Um." My throat feels like I've been gargling with gasoline.
"Who?"

"Randy? You know, you came into my office that day and introduced yourself as the new VFW Commander? Remember?"

"Oh, right." I rub my eyes, trying to wake up. I do remember now. This was the guy who didn't know the VFW existed, even though it was down the street from his nonprofit office. "How did you get my number?"

There was a pause. "Wow you sound tired, man. I figured I'd call early before you got busy with all that walking, you know. How's that going, by the way? You walking tall?"

I sit up. "Well, I'm not walking anywhere right now. It's five in the morning."

"Oh, sorry man. But early bird gets the worm, right? Anyway, I was calling just to check in and see, uh, what you're planning to do with the money you raise on the Go Fund Me." Before I fell asleep last night, I checked the Go Fund Me for VetZero on my phone and it still only had about a thousand dollars in it – and I think half of that (allegedly) came from my parents. So unless Bill Gates or the Sultan of Brunei have suddenly taken an interest in a fat guy walking across the country, the amount hasn't changed much over night. The goal is $40,387, to recognize the average number of veterans who are homeless every night in America, but that number seems so far away right now, on Day Three.

"So, your Go Fund Me page says you're donating the forty large to nonprofits in Poughkeepsie who help veterans." He actually uses those words, *forty large*, like he's Don Draper and we're filming an episode of *Mad Men*. If this guy starts pontificating on how advertising is based on happiness, I'm hanging up. "That's amazing – kudos to you, Tommy. I just wanted to ask, you know, how you're dividing that money out. Like, who is it going to, you know?"

"I haven't really figured that all out, Randy. I mean, I'm on day *three*."

"Oh I know, I know. Trust me, I know. Our nonprofit does a lot for the vets in Poughkeepsie. You know that, right? A lot. I can send you an email that shows how much we do for the veterans. It really spells it out."

"I got it, Randy. Thanks for the call."

"No problem. Hey before I let you go, any idea when you're going to hand that money out, when you get back?" I'll give it to him, this guy is definitely not bashful.

"No clue. I hope we reach our goal. But I appreciate the optimism, Randy."

"Hey, we're all in this together, right? Gotta take care of one another, that's my motto. One for one, all for all." He pauses. "Wait. One for *all*, all for *one*, I mean."

"Three Musketeers," I say with a little nostalgia, because it's actually one of my favorite books ever since I was a kid. That, and *Ivanhoe*. Hey, don't judge.

"Hey, do you want me to send you some *Three Musketeers* bars in the mail? Because I can do that, you know – no problem. I got you." I think Randy has somehow missed my 19th Century French literary reference.

"I'm good. Take it easy, Randy."

This oh-dark-early conversation with Randy turns out to be a bad omen for the rest of the day. On the plus side, Mark makes miraculous coffee with his old-school percolator pot, so I drink a couple of big mugs of this magic elixir as I scribble down my morning conversation with Randy. (In case, you know, I ever decide to write a book.) More good news: my legs are bouncing back a lot better than they did yesterday. They're still stiff as boards when I wake up, but this morning it only takes me a half-hour to stand up from the bed and step into the bathroom, under my own power.

Baby steps, I whisper up to Sister Mary. *Baby steps*.

Mark says I'm not allowed to pass through this part of Oregon without having breakfast at *The Shining* house. Apparently, the hotel where they filmed the movie is actually an ornate ski resort that sits at the top of a nearby mountain, a few miles up the road. *The Shining* was one of the movies that scared the bejeesus out of me as a kid, so who can say no to that? Breakfast is great (no ghosts or zombie children, or at least, none that I can see) but I'm preoccupied, listening to Mark tell me stories about his son in the Army. I can tell how proud Mark is of his son, which might explain why he tends bar at the VFW in Rhododendron. I try to pay for breakfast, but Mark won't allow it. "Least I can do," he says. "What you're trying to do is important to me."

Thanks, Mark. *Trying* being the key word there.

He drives us back down the ice-covered mountain in his little pickup and he drops me in front of the general store back in Rhododendron, where we say goodbye. There's a cold rain and it's about 34 degrees this morning. He says, "You got my cell, just in case." I smile bravely and I tell him I probably wouldn't need it, unless something really goes wrong.

Okay, something goes wrong. The walk today turns out to be pretty great, 21 miles total, although I have some trouble chugging up and down the hills. But the highway I'm following has a wide shoulder and the sun shows itself right around noon to warm me up a little – so all in all, I'm having a good day. My destination is a dot I saw on the Google map along Highway 26 called Clear Lake Campground, halfway between Rhododendron and the town of Warm Springs, on the enormous Warm Springs reservation.

I breathe a sigh of relief when I see the sign for the campground after a big bend in the road. Today's 21 miles has been rough, but not nearly as bad as that first day. Baby steps, baby steps. The campground sits on top of a rocky ridge, above the snow line. As I get closer to the turn-off, I start to get a little worried by the patches of snow I see here and there on the ground. It's about 70 degrees now with the sunshine, but we're above the snowline and my phone says the temperature will dip down to the 30s tonight. I'm hoping for the best. But as I turn the corner into the

campground parking lot – or at least, where the parking lot is supposed to be – my spirits sink like a stone.

There is a good four or five feet of packed ice and snow covering absolutely everything, including the entire parking lot. It's like
someone parked their glacier right here last night and then forgot about it. Okay, Google Maps, here's a complaint: please work
on adding a disclaimer that says *campground may be covered by
glacier.*

My first instinct is to just tough it out. How bad could it be?
Sure, you don't have one piece of the right equipment with you.
But you're a tough guy! You're a veteran! You once got stabbed in
the arm, in the Philippines! You fought a whole table of Marines at
the only bar in Guantanamo Bay! You dated a girl named Cha Cha
for six whole months, and lived to tell the tale!

You *got* this, kid!

But as soon as the sun starts to go down, I call Mark.

"I had a feeling you'd call," he said, almost laughing. "Snow up
there?"

"It's bad," I say, looking around at the winter wonderland.
"How did you know?"

"I've lived up here a long time. Doesn't really melt until July."
He's working at the VFW for another couple hours, but he agrees
to drive out and pick me up after his shift's over. This will be the
first in about a million times I will rely on the kindness of strangers as I fumble through the dark and try to keep going on this
walk across America. My feet feel surprisingly good so before it
gets completely dark, I bank a few more miles for tomorrow, while
waiting for my rescue. I'll stay at Mark's place for another night,
and in the morning he'll drive me right back up here to Glacier
Town to continue the walk along Highway 26 and into the Warm
Springs Reservation.

I have to admit, today I feel like a failure. It's only been three
days and already I feel completely overmatched, and completely

underprepared. I'm embarrassed. Nothing has gone according to plan. If not for Mark's kindness, the authorities might have found me frozen solid, weeks later. "Slept on top of a glacier," one deputy sighs to the other with a knowing nod. "I guess they'll never learn."

On the bright side, I'm relieved I get to sleep on an actual mattress tonight, instead of a bed of ice. I also get to enjoy two mornings in a row of Mark's percolator coffee. Hopefully Randy won't call again in the morning on Day Four, to check on the progress of that forty large.

Day 8

MILLICAN, OREGON

HERE'S THE short version of a seven-minute voicemail I accidentally butt-dialed to the Fiancée's phone, earlier this morning:

[At the tone, please record your message.] *I'm done! I'm done! Get the hell away from me! I'm so done. I'm done. I'm sick of this bullshit. Sick! No, it's bullshit. Am I right? Total bullshit. I just don't understand. I don't understand, okay? Listen,* [Unintelligible] *You hear me? No one cares. No one cares. You listen,* [Unintelligible] *I don't understand this. Get the hell away from me! Why? How is that even possible? Fuck that. No, no, fuck that. Ugh, I am done. Just leave me alone!* [End of Message]

So far, I've been keeping my iPhone in my thigh pocket as I walk, to count my steps more accurately; the only downside is, the phone bounces around and calls a random number, sometimes sending unintentional rants that sound like I'm yelling at the doctors while I try to escape from a psych ward. I'm eight days down on this walk and I think I've averaged one fluke message per day, including one to Mom. Thankfully, most of these messages have only recorded the mundane, muffled sounds of my heavy breathing – but today's butt-dial is a real masterpiece, a Tintoretto of lonely tirades, catching me in rare, desperate form.

Yup, it's only Day Eight and I'm already raving out here like a complete lunatic.

The Fiancée calls me right back, her voice trembling with fear and confusion after she listens to the whole seven minutes of calamity. "Who were you shouting at?"

"Myself," I sputter sheepishly. "God, maybe." I'm not a religious man, but I did spend thirteen years in Catholic school, so I do reserve the right to shout at God, whenever she's available for office hours. I say all this to the Fiancée in a feeble attempt to make her laugh, and maybe brush the whole thing off.

But she is not in a laughing mood this morning. "You frightened me, Tom. It sounded like you were being attacked."

"Nope, all alone out here," I say. "There *were* some hornets, a mile or so back."

"Well, you sounded absolutely crazy. I'm worried about you."

Much later, after the walk is over, I will listen to this message I left on her phone. I will cringe and close my eyes as I listen. It's clear I'm not complaining about being in any physical pain; I'm not complaining about the *how* of the walk. I'm complaining about the *why*, as in, why the hell are you still doing out here in the middle of nowhere? Why are you doing this in the first place? There's nothing really keeping you out here. Why don't you just go home?

Welcome back to the low road.

Today I'm walking the Millican Road south of Prineville, Oregon, and you know what, conditions are absolutely perfect: there's a clear blue sky, a dry 80 degrees that feels cooler with the soft breeze, and a flat, pristine highway ahead with a broad shoulder for easy walking and almost zero traffic in either direction. Even better, my feet are on the mend after a tortuous first week of pain, blood and blisters. Add the fact that I slept in an actual bed last night in Prineville, and this should definitely be one of the best days, ever. When I first imagined this walk in my head, today was pretty much the day I pictured, right down to the pixel.

So why am I raving out loud at myself and God? Why am I already resigned to quit this Quest for the Holy Fail after only eight days, and just go home?

Last night over some well-deserved Taco Bell in Prineville, I plotted my possible escape. Two more days walking south on the Millican Road will get me to US Route 20, the big highway that runs east-west all the way across Oregon. There's a truck stop there with a bus stop, so instead of turning east to continue the walk, I could just pick up the bus to Bend and then eventually find my way back to Portland. Then a quick flight back to New York, and *boom*, I slip unnoticed into my apartment in Poughkeepsie, pull the shades down, and stay there for the rest of the summer. Sounds like a plan. Maybe everyone would forget this half-baked idea by the time school started again on Labor Day. No harm, no foul. You gave it your best shot, kid.

After a week on the road, the physical part has actually started to become manageable. My middle-aged body is slowly acclimating to the shock of walking twenty-plus miles a day. My feet still swoon to the size of canned hams by the end of the day, but at least now I can wake up and make it to the bathroom on my own. Baby steps. Sure, I'm still sore, that's never going away. But the difference is, I'm getting used to that soreness, dealing with it, the same way we get used to crappy relationships: we do it over and over until the new normal feels like the old normal.

In that voice message I left by accident for the Fiancée, I don't hear a guy who's just doubting his broken-down, middle-aged body. I hear a guy who is doubting himself.

Look, I'll admit I didn't do as much physical training as I should have before this walk, but I did read a ton of books, trying to prepare myself for the mental challenge ahead. I read a tall stack of different books by men and women taking on quixotic challenges like mine; one of the best was a memoir called *Walking the Amazon* by a British Army veteran named Ed Stafford; it's got a blurb on the cover by none other than Bear Grylls, so when I saw it on the shelf at the Barnes & Noble, I figured it must be good. But as soon as I started reading, I got really discouraged – frightened, even – because the first fifty pages are just on the preparation Stafford and his team went through in order to get ready for their immense challenge. He even broke it down into a Nineteen Point Plan, with subtitles like *Evacuation Plan* and *Communications* and something called *Risk Assessment*. It sounded like Stafford had everything planned out, down to the last detail, before he even took his first step on his ambitious quest to travel the entire Amazon River on foot. Reading page after page about his pains-taking preparation gave me a queasy feeling inside.

Look, I have trouble just spelling *Risk Assessment*.

One thing that kept me reading Stafford's book until the end (he makes it!) was my curiosity about his reasons for taking on the challenge in the first place. Why was he doing it? As far as I can tell, Stafford simply wants to reach his destination to get acclaim in the Guinness Book of World Records. There was no real personal reason he was putting his life on the line in his foolhardy adventure, other than being the first and only person to make it to the finish line. That stuck with me, because for the whole length of the book, this guy is absolutely miserable. He's passing by amazing scenery that only a few humans will ever see with his head down, constantly focused on the finish line. As a result, he's constantly at wits end, and for what? A footnote in a record book? The whole thing seems empty to me; I'm impressed with how he conquers this amazing physical challenge, but I'm wondering about what pushed him to do it in the first place. It seems like his quest is heavy on detailing *Risk Assessment* but light on finding its soul.

I'm mulling over Stafford's book today as I walk through central

Oregon on my own quest, my head down, my feet beating the pavement while there is an endless postcard of beautiful scenery all around me, passing by at three miles per hour. The locals tell me this is called the high desert, and it's not what I thought Oregon would look like at all. Like everyone else in America, when I think of Oregon I picture the lush green forests and misty, snow-capped peaks like Mount Hood. Turns out most of the state doesn't look anything like that; when you leave the coast and cross the mountains heading east, the rest of Oregon is dry, rolling hills and scrub brush. But it's breathtaking and beautiful in its own way. I wish I could appreciate it, but I'm too busy moaning and complaining. And watching out for rattlesnakes.

Yesterday was Easter Sunday, so having a heart-to-heart with God seems appropriate. I'm wondering if I'll be able to pull off my own miracle and somehow rise from the dead and finish this walk, but the way I feel right now, it doesn't look good. My heart's not into it, and if I'm honest, it really has never been. Physically, I have to admit I am starting to feel pretty good – better than I had expected when I started this walk. But mentally? That's another story. Like Stafford, I know I am missing something.

There are no towns on this lonely road for the next two days, and definitely no motels, so I am pinning all my hopes for tonight on a sketchy Airbnb campsite I've found on my phone that allegedly is located on this road. The directions are simple: *take a right at the pink rock.* It's $30 a night for your very own campsite on the mountain, and the description all but guarantees you will see antelope. There were no customer reviews, though, which told me I might be the first, or the last person to see the antelope. Anyway, whether this place is real or just some virtual mirage, it's going to take 23 miles of walking today to get there, which would be my longest day so far.

I'm halfway into the day when I hear an engine coming in the opposite direction. Soon I see a plume of black smoke wafting in the distance. A tractor-trailer? Or with that loud rumble, maybe a tank? A couple of minutes later I see a beat-up Suburban rumbling down the two-lane highway. It's got more bondo than paint. It slows down and pulls up alongside me. "Well, howdy," the guy behind the wheel says to me in a slow, gruff voice. He's got a cigarette in his driving hand. "You must be the walker guy."

I'm surprised anyone knows who I am, especially out here. "How many walkers do you get on this road?"

"I've lived here forty years," he says. "And I believe you might be the first."

He introduces himself as Windhorse and tells me he runs the campsite I saw on Airbnb. "I'm running into Prineville for a few things. You like beef braciole?"

"You're talking to a guy who mostly eats at gas stations."

"Right," he says with a smoker's laugh. "It's the one dish I can cook."

"Sold. How much further to the pink rock?"

"About ten miles, give or take. There's a big steep hill right at the end, though. It's rough. I can pick you up on my way back, take you the rest of the way."

"Can't do that. I'm the walker guy, remember? I'm on a mission."

"A mission, huh? Sounds serious." His voice is dripping with sarcasm. He shakes his head and puts the car back in drive. "Okey-doke. Have it your way, amigo."

As I watch the rusty Suburban roll away in a cloud of exhaust, I can feel my face getting flushed with red, and it's more than just sunburn. Who does this guy think he is, making fun of me? And what kind of name is Windhorse, anyway?

I stew over this perceived slight for another four or five miles when I finally see the big hill, up ahead. Holy cow, he wasn't kidding about the steep incline. I drain my last water bottle for the day before I reach the top, when I hear the familiar chug of the Suburban closing behind me. "Meet you at the pink rock," he shouts out the window as he passes by. And sure enough, a few more miles and I spot a bright dash of flamingo up ahead. It's a rock painted Miami Vice pink, all right, and there's the rusty Suburban idling right behind it. "I'll give you a ride up the mountain," he says. "You can take the rest of the day off." Secretly I'm relieved. I can finally call it a day after 23 miles in the hot sun.

I climb into the passenger seat and dump my bag in the back. The inside of his truck looks a lot like mine, back home: soda cans, papers, old mail, and candy wrappers.

"My name's Tom," I say.

"I knew that," he said. "They got a picture of you in the local paper. That's how I knew you were the walker guy." I forgot I did a phone interview a few days ago with a weekly called the *Central Oregonian* – my first official press event from the road. Which appears to have elevated me to local celebrity status out here in the high desert, right below Wile E. Coyote and the Roadrunner.

We climb the dirt track that snakes its way up the side of the butte. I told Windhorse the story of my walking stick being lost. "That's a shame," he said. "You're gonna need that stick out here."

I laughed. "For the bears, right?"

"Mountain lions," he said. "You'll probably hear them tonight. Mating season. Sounds like a woman screaming."

"Are you serious?" I can't tell if he's being sarcastic behind the sunglasses and hat.

"Like a heart attack, amigo."

He drives me up to the top of the ridge where he's dug out maybe a half-dozen campsites from the brush, each with a fire ring and a water barrel. There's no one else here, as far as I can tell.

"You get many folks through Airbnb?"

"Well, I had some Germans come through last year," he says. "Bicyclers. Weren't used to sleeping outside, I think." I get the distinct feeling old Windhorse likes the high lonesome up here, all alone in his very own Fortress of Solitude, away from the crowded madness of a dicey world down below.

I drop my gear at the campsite and walk the quarter-mile back down the dirt trail to Windhorse's place. He's got a pretty sweet setup for himself. There's an old airstream trailer with a kind of enclosed porch built on the front. Across the clearing there's a little wooden workshop and in between there's a big herb garden, complete with one of those old wooden weathervanes. There's a few chickens pecking around in the garden, and once in a while I see a scrappy yip-dog dart in and out of the picture. Windhorse said something about a daughter, but everything I see up here points to a guy living alone on top of this remote butte for a long, long time.

We sit beside his garden on old weathered park benches, drinking coffee and smelling the meat simmering on his ancient Coleman stove. He's peppering me with a lot of pointed questions about the walk. Why are you doing it? How is this going to help veterans? What do you hope to achieve? He's putting me on the defensive. I don't really have any answers, but he keeps prodding me, making me feel uncomfortable. I'm a captive audience, up here on his mountain top. Soon the sun begins to dip behind the far ridge, casting long shadows around us.

I still don't know if he's pulling my chain about the mountain lions. He was right on the money about his cooking, though: the Italian beef he pulls off the propane stove is drowned in thick red wine and utterly delicious. I don't mention this to Windhorse, but I haven't eaten red meat in about sixteen years, due to gout. But I'm so hungry, I'd eat the logs burning in the fire right now. We both eat with our fingers and lick our thumbs, it's so good. The dog comes over and sits between us, waiting for his cut of the loot. As we eat, I notice the small silver pin stuck in Windhorse's floppy cowboy hat. I immediately recognize the sword and two crossed arrows as the symbol of the Green Berets; across the bottom of the pin is their slogan *De Oppresso Liber* – Latin for "Free the Oppressed."

When I see that, things start to make sense to me. Windhorse is a veteran. He wasn't being mean or condescending with all these questions. He was testing me.

But he isn't done with the interrogation. "The way I see it, amigo, you've got two choices: you do it for the journey, or you do it for the destination." What he means is, I'm either doing it for the experience, exploring every day out here for its own surprises, or else I'm doing it just to reach a goal, to make it all the way back home. "So here's my question for you: which one are you going to choose?"

I feel exposed. I can't give him a confident answer on why I'm doing this walk in the first place. Sure, I could talk his ear off on the *how* of walking this far, how my feet hurt, and how my body feels. But I feel embarrassed because I am eight days into this thing and I have never really thought about the *why*.

"You want a rifle?" he asks. "I wasn't kidding about the mountain lions."

"I'll take my chances." For a few seconds, I think that sounds pretty brave.

We say goodnight, and I follow the dirt track in the dark back to my little campsite and start a fire. The temperature is dropping rapidly, and all I have to fend off the cold is my thin VFW jacket and one of those mylar emergency blankets that only covers half my body. After an hour or so the fire begins to die down and I find myself lying alone in the darkness on the cold ground, watching my breath twirl in the ghostly moonlight. I have to walk another twenty miles in the morning, but it's too cold to sleep. I keep shivering. Around two in the morning, my phone reports it's a crisp 28 degrees out here.

And then I hear the mountain lions.

Two words immediately come to my lips: *Risk Assessment.*

Much later, when I am writing this book, I would look up Windhorse's claim that mountain lions sound like a woman screaming, when they are in heat. That turns out to be true, but I don't hear any of those screams tonight. What I *do* hear sounds like three or four house cats on steroids, in surround sound, as they seem to circle me. I quickly run out of wood for my feeble fire and basically stay frozen on the ground under my lame astronaut blanket until the sun starts to come up. With the cold and the predator party going on, I haven't managed one minute of sleep the whole night – and I'm supposed to walk another twenty miles today. I'm wondering what the world record distance for sleep-walking is right now – whatever the Guinness book says, I know I can break it.

This is already shaping up to be another horrible day, and I haven't even made it back to the highway yet. I'm hoping Windhorse's promised camp coffee can knock me back into place. When I mosey over to his trailer he's already working his magic on the camp stove, stirring up some scrambled eggs and filling the coffee percolator pot. The coffee definitely smells like salvation to a guy who didn't get any sleep last night. We eat eggs off paper plates and I'm drinking my coffee out of a metal mug that says *Fishing is For Me.*

Windhorse gets up and draws my attention to the edge of the garden, where he's got five or six walking sticks leaning against a railing. "I got one here should fit you," he says, picking up the longest one. "Hell, this should fit Paul Bunyan."

Windhorse seems like a different person this morning. He seems ... well, nicer. I thank him for the walking stick and test it out. It's a stout length of timber; I could have used it last night against the mountain lions.

The sun's starting to get hot and Windhorse offers to drive me back down to the main road. He stops the creaky truck half-way down the mountain and puts it in park. I wonder why we're stopping and to be honest, I'm a little scared. We sit there for what feels like hours before he says anything. "I'm going to tell you a story," he says with a deep breath. "It's my story."

Honestly, I have no idea what to expect. I rest my hand on the door handle, just in case this situation calls for an emergency exit. Windhorse takes off his dark sunglasses, and for the first time I can see his brilliant blue eyes.

"You ever hear of the Tet Offensive? Tet Mau Than?"

I nod. I know a little bit: the Tet Offensive was a massive campaign of surprise attacks by the Viet Cong in 1968 on South Vietnamese and American forces, all coordinated to occur on the holiday of Tet on January 30. Until this moment, it had always been a blip in the history books I'd read, but today, I am listening to a history lesson first-hand. I realize I am literally sitting next to history in this Suburban.

He tells me the story of his position being overrun by the enemy that morning. I sit there for twenty minutes, listening intently and not moving a muscle. I am not going to repeat his story here; I feel obliged to keep it safe, and keep it sacred. I get the feeling he hasn't told this story to anyone in a very long time. Maybe never. And I realize why this Vietnam veteran has holed up alone on top of this mountain in the middle of nowhere for the last forty years. We live in a world that's starting to believe nothing is sacred – but today, I am reminded that is simply not true. The stories of our veterans are sacred. Windhorse' story is sacred. Listening to him relive the past, I realize it's our duty to protect these stories as best we can, to pass on to future generations.

And just like that, this painful, stupid, foolhardy, vain, unnec-essary and chaotic walk becomes something totally different. It becomes worthwhile. Until now, I really had no clue why I was out here in the first place. With Windhorse's help, now I know. I'm out here because there are probably thousands of veterans just like Windhorse, tucked away in the hidden folds of America, isolated on back roads and lonely mountain tops. These are the veterans we will never see in the spotlight. These are the veterans whose stories we will never hear, unless someone chooses to get off the beaten path and meet these forgotten heroes on their own terms, face-to-face, and veteran-to-veteran.

That's not going to be an easy task for anyone, much less an overweight, middle-aged Navy vet with bad ankles and good intentions. It's a dirty job, walking the low road with a purpose. But today is the day I realize, somebody's got to do it. I have Windhorse to thank for that. We roll the rest of the way down to the main road in his battered old truck, where the pink rock marks my official starting line of another day on the trail.

Today the miles melt together surprisingly quickly, even with zero sleep last night on the cold ground while being serenaded by mountain lions. My mind is occupied by my encounter with Windhorse and the story he entrusted to me. It's around dinner-time when I limp into the Brothers truck stop on US-20. There's a little blink-and-you'll-miss-it bus stop sign on the side of the road; the guy inside tells me you have to flag it down. I check the bus schedule on my phone; if it's on time, today's westbound bus for Bend should roll by in about an hour. I sit down in a booth against the window, eating a meal of marble cake and Reese's peanut butter cups washed down with three big Gatorades. I'm keeping an eye out for that bus as I watch the highway traffic outside. I'm still thinking about what Windhorse said about choosing the journey, or the destination. After an hour or so, I'm still sitting inside while I watch the bus – a big van, really – cruise by without stopping, headed west towards its final destination of Bend, Oregon. Me, I've decided I'm here for the journey. I'm here for the now. And for the first time out here, I'm excited to explore.

In fiction workshop at Marist, we talk a lot about epiphany

driving a character-driven story. If you want your story to be truly about character instead of plot, the theory goes, you must put your character through some kind of emotional trauma, a fire, and then see what happens when she or he comes out the other end. Have they learned anything? Have their lives changed? That change in the character is called the epiphany.

Here's the thing: you have to build up to it gradually; epiphany has to be earned, and as a result, most novels, memoirs, movies (and anything else with a story) normally have their epiphany at the very end, or close to it. It's what we expect from our stories these days.

We're only on Day 8 of this story, and already we've got the epiphany. It's not supposed to happen like that. It's not following the rules. In other words, if a student handed in this story draft for my fiction workshop, it would probably get a C+. (Okay, maybe a B- with the effort.) I mean, the hero hasn't even peed himself yet. Or run out of water.

See? I told you this book wouldn't be anything like *Eat, Pray, Love*.

Day 12

DREWSEY, OREGON

Damn. I think we've reached the part of the book where I'm supposed to tell you more about myself. Trust me, that's not my idea; I'd be happy to stick to telling stories from the road the whole time, with a few more corny jokes thrown in for good measure. But this is a memoir, after all, and I've been told by various smart people who know memoirs that I'm definitely supposed to talk about myself. "Treat it like a first date," one smart person told me. If this book was a first date, we'd be about a half-hour into the date right now, finishing our apps and ordering our second drink – or maybe our fifth drinks, depending on how bad the date's going. If you're under thirty and you have no idea what a "date" is, Google it; people ate food at the same table, they opened doors for one another, they kissed on doorsteps and then called each other 6-12 days later. Yes, it was an outrageous time. Anyway, there's always that uncomfortable silence right after they take those little appetizer plates away. You know what I'm talking about. We'll desperately try to fill the void by blurting out a story about ourselves, something pithy but not too pithy; something funny but not like, funny *weird*. Not Fozzie Bear funny, either – just enough enthusiasm to keep their attention, but not enough to make them call the cops.

Most memoirs seem to take a time-out right around this same point, too, don't they? At least, the ones I've read sure do. The first few chapters engage us with the action right away, and then *boom*, there's a quick detour into the serious stuff, the deep stuff. The uncomfortable stuff. They tap the brakes by circling back to some unresolved trauma in the writer's life, digging up vital clues from their past to help the reader better understand the present. It's usually a vivid childhood memory, or maybe a more recent story about abuse or a bad breakup – but either way, it's some-thing that's been fueling a fire inside the author for a long time. The reader feels more empathy for the person because now we've seen them naked, so to speak, warts and all. We're allowed to see their flaws and imperfections, and it makes us keep reading until the end.

That's the power of a good memoir, and I think it's really the main reason we read good memoirs: to see inside someone else's twisted life, and compare it to our own. A good memoir can inspire us to do better, and to be better; a good memoir must be honest and raw. And if you're trying to write one, I have been told, you'd better be prepared to get honest and raw about yourself. Otherwise, it won't work. We don't read memoirs for the story. We read memoirs to experience the story beneath the story.

Fair enough. But what do you do when you're supposed to write a memoir about yourself, and you're not really prepared to write about yourself? What do you do when you have to let people in, but you don't know how?

Aye, there's the rub.

Long after this walk is over, I will email a rough draft of the Prologue of this book to my sister-in-law, looking for feedback. She's one of those smart people who know memoirs because she's actually a very successful literary agent in New York City. I have a growing suspicion she feels sorry for me, since my first three novels sold a grand total of twelve copies; but she married my little brother, so I guess she might feel the same. (Sorry, John.)

Seriously, didn't we *just* say, no Fozzie Bear humor? Sheesh.

Anyway, I will get her reply as I'm writing this very chapter on Day 12 -- that sure was fast! And she writes: *it reads a bit jokey. I think I need to feel a bit more of your earnestness and truth. It needs more heart and emotion and character development to make the reader invested and see ourselves in you. Like WILD for example. Here, the humor feels like an evasion to me.*

Well put, sis. You are 100% right, and I truly appreciate the tough love.

But I'm also like, heart and emotion? Did you NOT READ the part in the Prologue about peeing myself in the fifth grade? Geez, I feel like Russell Crowe out here. "ARE YOU NOT ENTERTAINED?" But if there's any silver lining to her tough love, it's that my sister-in-law who is a bigtime literary agent mentioned Cheryl Strayed's landmark memoir *WILD* in the same breath as my almost-book! (Hey, admit it, she did write: *like WILD.*) So as a result, I'll drink heavily and when I wake up I will remember her tough-love email as saying, *your book is like WILD.* Hey, don't judge! Writing is hard. It's like I tell my students: you've got to grab inspiration wherever you can find it. Even if you have to totally make it up yourself.

Here's a detour: in my writing workshops at Marist, one of the first things we learn is every character has a tragic flaw. You've heard this one before, I'm sure: Achilles had his heel, Ahab had his whale, Luke Skywalker had his father – and for me, it's apparently talking about myself. I mean, we're about to reveal what happens on Day 12, a very important chapter in the overall arc of this book if I do say so myself. It feels like we're turning circles. It feels like we're knee-deep in that uncomfortable silence of our first date, as

we wait for someone to share some embarrassing personal anec-
dote so we can move on and get back to the good part.

I have to say, this is all very frustrating, this memoir-writing
business. I guess we're too far into this thing to turn back now. So
let's order another drink and get back to the good part of this book
already. Let's get back to the walk.

I know the title page for this chapter says Day 12 takes place
around Drewsey, Oregon but honestly, it's a guess: I have no idea
where I am when I reach Rusty's run down farm. I know I'm in
Harney County, because a mile or so back there's a sign that reads
HARNEY COUNTY – ONION CAPITAL OF THE WORLD. Good
to know. If the next county over boasts it's the cheesesteak capital of the world, well, I'll know I walked off the Google maps and
straight into heaven. I'm tired of dodging the constant oncoming
traffic on a bustling US-20, so I check my phone to find an alternate route. I'm in luck: the map says there's a railroad access road
coming up that runs parallel to the highway. More or less. I pass a
historical marker for the Old Oregon Trail – they're strewn along
this highway every so often, promising wheel ruts and abandoned
camp grounds from the original settlers – and take the plunge onto
a dirt road that dips away from the main road, into the wilderness.

There's both good and bad news when you want to escape the
hustle and bustle of the main road and instead, try your luck and
walk the road less traveled. The good news, of course, is fewer
trucks to dodge, less diesel in your lungs, and less grit thrown in
your face by oncoming traffic. Let's face it, America is definitely not
made for walking. America is made for driving, and thru-walkers
have to stay alert just to stay alive.

The bad news about taking a back road, instead? The dogs.
Lots and lots of dogs! Farm dogs, yard dogs, stray dogs, and
honest-to-goodness junkyard dogs. Out here in rural America,

I'm pretty sure there are more dogs than people. Now, all these dogs living off the beaten path have never actually seen a human walking on their road, so they get very excited when they spot you. It's like they're seeing Jesus walk by, if dogs could recognize Jesus. They bark loud enough for dogs living three counties over to get excited about the news: *he's coming, he's coming, he's coming!* Back on Day 4, I had a big Malamute run off a porch on the Warm Springs reservation and stalk me for a good six miles before its owner drove up and took them back home. And on Day 5 an excited front-yard dog bit my ankle! Luckily the rubber in my Walmart ankle braces is too thick for dog teeth to puncture; I think that's what it actually says on the package, right after the washing instructions. After the walk is over, I will hold onto that brace, just to show the teeth marks and tell the story. The dog gets a lot bigger, every time I tell it.

So, to recap the conundrum of walking across America: it's either trucks or dogs.

The lady, or the tiger. You can certainly pick your poison, out here on the low road.

It's around three in the afternoon on Day 12 when I come up on an abandoned farm. At least, it looks abandoned: there's an old farmhouse hiding behind a big weeping willow but the place looks boarded up. There's also a single-wide trailer with a lopsided porch sitting closer to the road, but honestly, it doesn't look much more inviting. Behind the house there's an unkempt, fallow field that goes on and on. I can smell the onions. I'm tired; the sun is high in the sky and I've already been Jesus to three different farm dogs today. When I get close in on the trailer by the side of the road, I hear more barking, but the weeds are so high, I can't see anything moving. *Great*, I think. *Cujo started just like this.* I speed up my pace, trying to put some safe distance between me and whatever is barking from the weeds. Then I finally see a flash of white fur burst out onto the road in front of me, closing fast.

"Watch out for Zooey," a voice shouts from the crooked porch. "She might lick you to death."

Turns out I don't have to worry about Zooey at all. She's a tiny dog, a Jack Russell maybe, and a real sweetheart. She gallops in circles around me a few times, her tongue hanging out the whole time. She's having a ball making herself dizzy; I'm getting dizzy just trying to keep my eye on her, so I stop. She stops too. We smile at each other.

"Yeah," I yell back to the guy on the porch. "She's a real killer."

"Hold on a minute," he yells, ducking inside the trailer for a moment while Zooey stands guard next to my leg, tail whipping back and forth. The guy comes back out with a cold bottle of water. I can see he has a lot of trouble walking. "Hot day to be walking," he says, handing me the water. "You lost?"

I tell him the elevator version about the walk, and why I'm doing it. He perks up the moment I say the word *veterans*. "Hey, I'm a vet. My son, too. Both Army. How far you got to go?"

"Poughkeepsie," I say, draining the bottle in one gulp. "It's in New York."

"No shit?" Rusty says, lowering his tea shades to gaze down the empty road behind me. "You got anyone following you?"

"Just me," I say.

"No shit." We stand there talking for a while, sharing stories: Rusty tells me about his time in the Army back in the 1980s as a Horizontal Construction Engineer, driving big rigs and dozers, and I tell him a little about my time in the Navy, floating around the Persian Gulf in the 1990s.

"I got out right before that whole Gulf thing started," he says. "Wrecked my back, and then got drummed out on a medical. Really sad I never made it over there. All my buddies did." I can hear a lifetime of regret in his raspy voice.

"You didn't miss much, trust me." I say, trying to make him feel better. "Hundred and twenty in the shade over there, every day."

"Shit." Then Rusty tells me the rest of his story: how he came back here to his family farm after the Army, got married and had a son, but his back never got better and after a while he couldn't do the work needed around the farm. Then he got divorced, his son got discharged, and now it's just the two of them living in this little trailer on the edge of a huge property. "Rheumatoid arthritis," he says. "What a bitch."

I don't tell Rusty this, but I know so many guys like him back home at the VFW; guys around my age or maybe a just little older who move like they're made out of popsicle sticks or peanut brittle. It's a common tale for veterans: your body gets chewed up in the service, then you get discharged on a disability and now, years and years later, you're still trying to put Humpty Dumpty back together again. If there's one thing that veterans have in common, it's pain. That makes me angry, and it should make you angry, too. I'm waking up to the reality that we don't take care of our veterans in America nearly as good as we should. And I guess I'm out here taking my lumps on the low road to wake up other folks like you to this sad but undeniable truth. Rusty's story about not being able to get the medical care he needs from the VA is a common one, but that doesn't make the story any less heartbreaking, each time you hear it.

Rusty tells me his son is 27 years old but recently got a medical discharge from the Army, too, for mental health issues. He lives in the trailer now with Rusty. "He's inside right now, doing his video games," Rusty says. "He's got 100% disability for PTSD. We both got 100%, but that don't matter much when the closest VA hospital is all the way over in Boise. My son's not allowed to drive, and most days, my back won't let me drive that far. So we're kinda screwed." Later, I will look up the distance and he's absolutely right, Boise is more than 100 miles drive, each way. "Honestly, I worry about him more than me. Sometimes he comes out and mows the lawn," Rusty says. "He likes the mower."

As if on cue, I see a younger guy in shorts and a t-shirt with the sleeves ripped off come out of the trailer and saunter over to a riding mower parked in front of the old farmhouse. He starts it up, pushes down the bale handle and starts turning slow circles in the mangy lawn. Rusty and I watch him work as we talk for a few more minutes over the buzzing sound of the mower. I thank him for the water and ask him if we can take a picture together for Facebook. "I'm on the Facebook," Rusty says approvingly. "I'll have to check it out." He asks me if I'm going to write a book about the walk, after I get back home.

"I hope so," I say. "If I do, you'll be in it, for sure."

That's the thing about veterans: when you meet a fellow vet for the first time, it takes all of fifteen minutes before you feel like you've known that person your whole life. There's an invisible bond there, for sure. Ask any veteran, and they'll no doubt agree – well, except for Marines. Marines hate everybody.

Just kidding, Marines!

I'm about a half-mile farther down the road when I hear a motor behind me. Sure enough, it's Rusty in a four-wheeler, with Zooey riding shotgun. "Brought you some more water," he says, handing me three or four more bottles to stash in my mailbag. I get the feeling he doesn't want to see me go, just yet. He putters alongside me for another hundred yards or so, pointing out a few local landmarks in the distance. I'm afraid to ask when the last time someone else walked past their farm, but I'm guessing it was a long time ago.

"There's an irrigation culvert that runs all the way through there," Rusty says, pointing to the field. "We used to ride dirt bikes up and down there, every day after school. I had this little Yamaha 80 GT. We built our own jumps." He stops the four-wheeler and looks around with an air of nostalgia. "Not such a bad place to grow up."

"Fucking A," I say, nodding. "Onion capital of the world."

He laughs. "You got it." He's about to turn the cart around and head for home, but he stops alongside me for a moment instead. "Thank you for what you're doing," he says, lowering his shades so I can see his eyes. "It means a lot to me." We shake hands firmly and say some more goodbyes. I say goodbye to Zooey, too, but now she's acting very nonchalant, as if she's fully expecting to see me walk by again tomorrow, and the next day, and the next, in her own dog version of the movie *Groundhog Day*.

Later that night, as I'm writing in my journal about my encounter with Rusty, I have another epiphany. I realize this memoir isn't about me. I realize this isn't my story, after all.

This story really belongs to all the veterans I'm meeting on this journey. There's so many who seem lost in America. My name might be on the cover, but this is Rusty's book. This feels like Windhorse's story a whole lot more than it feels like mine. This belongs to the construction foreman who saved me on a 100-degree day in Warm Springs. It belongs to veterans like Bob in Burley (you'll meet him soon) and Chris in Mountain Home (him, too) and the female vet I talked with outside Beloit, Wisconsin who wouldn't give me her name. This book is property of all the veterans I will meet outside gas stations and inside bars all across America. This book is owned by every veteran in America who feels lost, alone, or adrift in an increasingly worrisome world. This is your book.

So for now, I'm going to think of this book as ... an anti-memoir. It's the exact opposite of what I started out to write, because now I realize my purpose out here is not to tell my story but instead, listen to the amazing stories of others. My goal on this journey is to meet as many fellow veterans as I can and just listen to their stories – and as far as I know, there's only one way you can listen to veterans like Windhorse and Rusty and countless others who live on the roads less traveled in America. No, driving by in your SUV and sending an email ain't going to cut it. You have to seek these folks out and meet them, eye to eye. You have to walk a little on the wild side. You have to take a risk and get chased by dogs out on the low road.

When I find the highway again, every so often I will pass a little brown historical marker which promises some visible wagon ruts located nearby, left by the original pioneers of the Old Oregon Trail; being a curious student of American history, I almost always investigate. Before the transcontinental railroad was completed in 1869, about 400,000 Americans struggled and slogged along a twisted web of dirt tracks from St. Louis all the way to Portland. It was a difficult road west, with as many as 21,000 of those travelers succumbing to everything from drownings to scurvy. Whenever I find their preserved wheel-ruts cut into the hard dirt on the side of the paved road, I am reminded of how tough these settlers must have been, to make it this far on foot. These men and women had to carry everything they needed for the entire journey. They ate hardtack and wild berries. They made their cooking fires with buffalo chips. They slept outside. They didn't even consider turning back. They shared a common pain in overcoming incredible obstacles, but they also shared the same passion for the promise of a better life ahead.

We are following the same path in opposite directions, but their story feels so much bigger than mine, and much more significant. When I think about all they went through to make it this far on the trail, somehow my own problems seem a bit smaller, and my feet don't hurt quite as much.

Buffalo chips? Yikes. And I thought I smelled bad.

I stand on the side of the road for a few minutes, fitting the sole of my shoe into the marks they left behind, looking for things left behind, listening for ghosts.

Day 22

BOISE, IDAHO

W HEN I finished my graduate degree at the University of Alabama in 2002, my mentor presented me with an oar. Yes, an actual oar, the six-foot long hunk of wood you'd use to row, row, row your boat, gently down the stream. At writing programs, it's customary to receive a gift from your thesis advisor after you pass your defense, but it's usually a book or an antique pen or something else writerly; so at the time, I thought the oar was some kind of gag gift, or worse, an inside joke about my writing – as in, *your writing style's about as subtle as hitting folks over the head with an oar, Zurhellen* – or something like that. But no, he didn't mean it as a joke or insult all, and knowing Michael Martone the way I do now almost twenty years later, I should have been paying better attention at the time. If you know the eminent writer and teacher Michael Martone, too, then I don't have to tell you that when he decides to give you something, there's bound to be a story behind it. And a good one, at that.

Martone was (and is) a great mentor for me and so many other writers, and I owe him a lot. When I showed up at Alabama with not much more than a dollar and a dream, he kind of took me under his wing and showed me how to take this whole writing thing seriously, but not too seriously. He also knew I was a Navy veteran, and I'm pretty sure they don't see many vets enrolled in high-falootin' M.F.A. writing programs like this one. At least, I sure didn't see any other veterans while I was there.

"This is the perfect gift for an old sailor," he told me as he handed me the oar outside his office in Morgan Hall. His face was beaming with excitement.

I took it in both hands and stared at it, up and down. Looking back, I don't think I masked my disappointment very well. After all, I knew he gave my buddy Buckbee a big gallery book about Ansel Adams, and he gave my other buddy Baker (Baker actually shows up later in this very same chapter, in Boise!) another cool book about how kudzu took over the American South. Me, I got an oar.

"It's an oar," I said. At least I knew the difference between an oar and a paddle. "Oh, it's not just an oar," Martone said. "This is so much more than just an oar."

I didn't say anything; I was waiting for Martone to chant some magic words and turn this big chunk of wood into something much more than an oar, like a dragon or a chest of doubloons or even better, the gas money I was going to need to drive the thousand miles up to New York after graduation.

"This is the winnowing oar, from the Odyssey," he told me, patting the polished wood of the oar like it was made out of solid gold. He took the blank stare on my face in stride. "Look it up. Odysseus was an old sailor trying to make it home, just like you."

"Winnowing oar," I said with a yawn. "Got it."

"Trust me, Tommy, you're going to need this someday. Don't lose it."

Oh, I wasn't worried about losing it. I was more worried about fitting this giant toothpick into my soft-top Jeep with all the other gear I was taking home. I couldn't leave it behind, simply because I respected the guy way too much. Maybe I could stand it straight up in the back of my Jeep, stick a sail on it, and have the wind push me all the way back to New York.

It's been collecting dust in my office at Marist College ever since, lurking in a corner next to the coat rack. Whenever students see the oar they always ask, "Why do you have that?" For years I would just tell them it was a gift, and leave it at that. But when I started thinking about this whole VetZero Walk Across America idea, I remembered what Martone said about Odysseus and the winnowing oar, so I browsed my copy of Homer's epic poem, looking for a quick shot of inspiration.

Apologies, Martone. I should have looked this up a long time ago.

At the end of the Odyssey, after Odysseus has returned home to Ithaca and slaughtered all the suitors, he tells his wife Penelope his quest is not yet over. (She hasn't seen her man in fifteen years, so understandably, she's a little pissed.) Earlier in the story, Odysseus meets the oracle Tiresias in the Underworld and asks the blind seer, *How will I know when my quest has finally ended?* Tiresias tells him that after he returns home, Odysseus must carry an oar from his ship on a walking journey far inland, until he comes to a country where the people don't recognize the oar since they've never even heard of ships or the sea. At the moment a stranger asks if that's a winnower (basically an old-school farming shovel or fork) Odysseus is carrying on his shoulder, he should immediately stick the oar in the ground and make a sacrifice to the gods.

Then, and only then, Tiresias informs him, his epic quest will be done and he can finally return home, to live out the rest of his long life in peace, by the sea.

Holy metaphor, Batman!

Okay, I knew Martone was a great teacher and mentor, but back at Alabama I had no idea he also had the power to see into the future, just like Tiresias! How else could he know that many years later in 2019, I would find myself on my own Odyssey, another old sailor walking inland, trying desperately to find the way home?

Literary nerds (like me!) know the poet T.S. Eliot shared Homer's sentiment when he wrote, *the end of all our exploring will be to arrive where we started, and know the place for the first time.* In other words, we have to go out and explore the world in order to find home. We have to see the world from every possible angle before we can find ourselves. We have to push ourselves out of our comfort zones to find the person we're really supposed to be, getting deep into some "good trouble" as that great American hero John Lewis once said.

Needless to say, this discovery instantly energized me when I was trying to get the courage up to somehow walk across America alone. And now, as I struggle to lay down the structure of this book, I find it easy to parallel the story of Odysseus' walk with my own – so much so that if you notice the epigraph of this book, it's actually the opening lines to the Odyssey itself. All because my grad school mentor gave me a kooky gift back in the day.

Well played, Michael Martone. Well played, indeed.

My all-time favorite quote from the Odyssey seems especially pertinent right now: "A man who has been through bitter experiences and travelled far enjoys even his sufferings after a time." In other words, if you go far enough, you get used to the pain. You actually start to depend on it, to keep you going.

Today is Day 22 and I'm imagining myself as Odysseus and my big walking stick as his oar as I limp into the downtown area of Caldwell, Idaho and collapse into a coffee shop's fluffy couch after a slow but solid twenty-mile day on the road. I don't know what the ancient Greeks did for a twisted ankle in the middle of a quest – they probably stopped, sacrificed a goat, and asked the gods for a miracle. The fact I'm still on my feet on Day 22 is a small miracle in itself, especially since I wrecked my right ankle on some loose gravel a couple days ago. Walking wounded, indeed. Even with the bum ankle, I know I'm lucky to make it this far. But I feel my luck is going to run out sooner than later if I don't make some big changes.

From the couch, I order the coldest coffee drink they have and dig out my phone to call my old shipmate Jeff, who lives nearby in Nampa. I haven't seen Jeff in more than twenty years, but I'm excited to see him. We were in the Navy together, both working out of the electrical shop on the nuclear cruiser USS *California* back in the 1990s. He's always been a good friend, but even more important right now, Jeff teaches an outdoor survival course here in the Treasure Valley, so I'm positive he'll know exactly what gear I'll need. At the very least, I know I can expect a little support and sympathy from an old shipmate.

"You look like shit," Jeff says when I pour myself into his pickup outside the coffee shop. So much for that sympathy. We pick up speed and head back into the traffic starting to choke downtown Caldwell in the afternoon rush hour.

When you haven't sat in a car for three weeks, much less drive one, you get a little freaked out at how fast everything is moving around you. The world looks a lot different at three miles an hour, after all. As we pull onto Caldwell's main drag, I start talking like a great-grandma: *whoa, slow down, we're going way too fast.* It feels like we're flying at a hundred miles an hour, and at intersections, I get even more nervous, my head on a swivel to avoid getting hit by oncoming traffic.

"Slow down," I say as we turn onto a two-lane highway and pick up speed.

"We're going twenty-seven miles an hour right now," Jeff says, lifting his driving hand to check the gage. "The speed limit is 45."

"It just feels fast. Okay, you got a truck up there. Look out."

"Where?"

"*There*," I say, pointing out a delivery van maybe a quarter-mile ahead.

"It's parked," he sighs. The tone of his voice must be the same when he's talking to his three-year old. "There's no one in it. And it's on the other side of the divider."

I shrug, my eyes still darting around, on the lookout for trouble. "It looked like it was moving."

"You need a beer," Jeff says. "A beer and a doctor, for that ankle. Maybe not in that order." He points to a little blue cooler in the back seat. "I'll stay off I-84 on the way home today. You've been here five minutes, don't want to give you a fucking heart attack."

Jeff is a power systems draftsman for Idaho Power, which means he draws the plans for any business or homeowner who wants power across the Treasure Valley. He drives a lot from jobsite to jobsite. He works with a couple of other guys I know from EM shop on the *California*, Shayne and Eric. We all got discharged around the same time; I stayed in the Seattle area to give grad school a try, and the three of them moved to Boise to work for Idaho Power twenty years ago, settling down and raising their families in a great, up-and-coming area of the country to live. Jeff and his wife Abby have three little girls; he tells me he's hooked up their travel camper in the driveway, so I can have my own space tonight.

"By the way, Shayne called the TV news, they're sending a reporter out to my house tonight around six to do an interview with you."

Hey, my first TV interview! "Wow, I didn't know I was such big news in Boise."

"You're not," Jeff says. "Shayne had to call and pitch it to like, seven stations."

As promised, a young reporter and her cameraman are waiting cheerily outside Jeff's house when we pull up around six. I'm ready for my close-up. They take me out to the access road outside the development, to get footage of me walking on the shoulder towards the camera. Then, walking away from the camera. Then, walking towards and then turning and walking away from the camera. Then, walking past the camera on the ground so it gets my feet this way. Then the other way. Later I will learn this is what they call the B-Roll footage. All in all, they take about a half-hour worth of video for what will ultimately be a thirty-second story tacked onto the end of tonight's late news, as they roll the credits and say good-night.

Shayne comes over after work and the three of us sit around Jeff's kitchen table, drinking a few beers and telling stories. I had forgotten a few of them, and I have to say, it's great catching up with these guys. I haven't really had a conversation with anyone since I came across Rusty and Zooey back in Oregon, and besides, talking about the old times always feels good. That's one thing about veterans: it's a lot easier sharing these stories with other veterans than it is trying to explain them to civilians. You don't have to fill in the blanks, because veterans all speak the same common language. Shayne and Jeff pepper me with a lot of questions about the walk, too. They can't believe I made it this far – 400 miles from the start back in Portland.

Shayne goes home after a couple hours, but we'll see him tomorrow on the walk into downtown Boise. Jeff digs out a pad of paper and a pen and throws them down on the table in front of me. "Write this down," he says, and he goes into a long list of everything I'll need on the walk, everything from a lightweight backpack to a first aid kit. I can tell he's in his element; he's rattling off the weight of each item, down to the ounce. Tomorrow we'll get up early and hit the local camping megastore to pick up everything on my new list. "It's right next to the Cracker Barrel," he says. "So everyone wins."

Jeff looks over the list one last time before we finally call it a night. He makes a couple of notes in the margins and then finally gives it a nod of approval. "It's a *whole new world*," he says, suddenly bursting out full-throttle into the old Disney song. "Now you'll be ready for anything, brother." He looks at my face, which is frozen in genuine surprise. "What?"

"Nothing. I've never heard you sing before."

"Hey, when you're Dad to three little girls," he says. "You better be able to sing."

When I started, I thought I had this walk all figured out. While I was planning everything right down to the last foolproof detail, I honestly imagined I'd look something like Caine in that old TV show *Kung Fu*, just a guy gliding alone across the Earth in search of meaning. I also visualized myself as David Banner in *The Incredible Hulk*; I figured if he could walk around the country for five whole seasons with nothing but a windbreaker and a shoulder bag, then I could make it across America once. I planned to rely on my phone for just about everything, from counting my daily steps to finding the right route. I had plans to listen to great music, great books, and great podcasts the whole time. I had made a dozen playlists, each for just the right moment: uphill, downhill, sunrise, sunset. I had read hundreds of online reviews. I had done hours and hours of research on the best apps to download to my phone, including one called *Flush* that lets you know where the nearest public toilet is located. Like any teacher worth their weight in chalk, I wrapped myself in the research, hoping this would prepare me for any situation.

We all know that old saying, attributed to Julius Caesar: experience is the best teacher of all. Every day I spend out here on the low road, I want to amend it, to do old JC one better: experience isn't the best teacher, it's really the only teacher. At least, that's how it feels out here. I've spent most of my life in one school or another, training to become a college professor, but I feel like I've learned more about the world (and myself) in just the last three weeks of walking the walk.

When I crossed the Snake River into Idaho two days ago, I realized I wasn't prepared for *anything* out here on the low road. I had all the wrong gear, but even worse, I had the wrong attitude. Windhorse proved that to me. When I reach Boise tomorrow I will have walked 400 miles so far – and considering how wrong everything has been so far, that in itself is a complete miracle.

So far, I haven't listened to anything on my phone; turns out, when you're walking along a highway, you want to hear the trucks coming. And when you're on the back roads, you want to hear the dogs coming, too. So basically, I've been forced to sing to myself the whole time, to stave off boredom. Which sounds harmless, but a few days ago my good friend Dayna sent a video, introducing me to some fresh piece of Hell called "Baby Shark" and now, I can't get that damned song out of my head. *Doo doo-doo doodoo*!

It's also clear I brought the wrong shoes for this kind of work. I've got these expensive lightweight running shoes with a ton of cushioning, which is perfect for walking around a high school track but they're useless out here. There's zero ankle support and little traction; both are vital when you're trying to scramble on a soft shoulder at an angle. Two days ago, I twisted my ankle pretty bad when I hit a rough patch of gravel, and even though I'm icing it when I can, it's not getting any better. It balloons up when I get off my feet, but after an hour or so walking it calms down enough to forget about it. The ankle braces and ibuprofen seem to help. The Fiancée sent a CBD oil stick to help with the swelling, but I keep it hidden since I'm not sure Idaho law enforcement has caught up with the rest of the country, yet.

The young guy at the camping store has helped Jeff outfit his survival classes for years, but when Jeff tries to explain what I'm doing here today, the kid isn't buying it. His nametag says *Oakley* and he keeps tapping the Bluetooth in his ear while they talk, as if seeking answers from a higher authority. I think they've both forgotten I'm standing right here. "So, he walked from where?"

Jeff smiles. "Portland, Oregon."

"Uh *huh*. To Boise?"

"Yup. That's 400 miles."

"Okay. And he's trying to get to where?"

"Poughkeepsie."

"Uh huh. And where is that?"

"New York. It's about 2,400 miles away. Give or take."

"Okay." He processes it for a moment. "And what kind of gear is he looking for?"

That's when Jeff lets out a big laugh. He pulls the list out of his jeans pocket with a dramatic flair, whipping it a couple times in the air like a fancy napkin and then hands the crumpled paper over to the kid. "Dude hiked 400 miles alone so far," Jeff says. "Without *any* of this stuff."

Oakley scans the list and then looks up at me. Now he's got a big smile, too. "Holy SHIT," he says, way too loud: everyone in the store looks over, including the older woman behind the customer service desk. She must be in charge here, and she does not look happy.

Oakley taps his earpiece again. "Yeah, sorry about that, Jennette. Uh huh. Okay. Okay, but listen, I got a guy here walking all the way across the country with like, running shoes and a mailbag. No, I'm not kidding. Nope. Nope, doesn't have that, either. Yeah, this dude right here," he says, standing next to me like he's MC of a beauty pageant. I wave half-heartedly over to Jennette, but she looks back with her hand over her mouth like she's watching a horror movie, the scary part where the monster sneaks up on the clueless guy lost in the woods.

"Pow-keep-see," Oakley says into the mic, shrugging his

shoulders. "Yeah, I don't know either. Okay. Yeah, I will." He looks at the list again and lets out a low whistle. Then he starts to walk backwards towards the stairs that lead to the tent village (there's a tent village) and he motions for us to follow. "Jennette says good luck."

By now, Jeff's face has turned beet red, his eyes closed as he laughs up a lung. "*Shut up*," I whisper.

After an hour, I escape my FNG Hell of Camping World. (If you're not familiar with the acronym FNG, just ask any vet. Not a compliment.) I'm down about a thousand dollars and most of my dignity, but the good news is after 400 miles I've finally got the right gear and some basic knowledge on how to use it. And we're also walking across the parking lot to eat at the Cracker Barrel, so life can't be that bad.

It's crowded inside this morning but we score a table up front by the windows. I'm hungry. I had a good sleep last night in the trailer parked in Jeff's driveway. Our server comes over and we chat a little; her brown apron is embroidered in gold with three stars and her name, *Doris*. I'm thinking this must be some sort of lucky sign about the walk.

Which makes it official: I know I have to order the catfish.

I can't believe I haven't mentioned Doris in this book yet! Not this Doris who works at the Cracker Barrel in Caldwell, Idaho – no, my good friend Doris who lives back in Poughkeepsie. My Doris is ninety-seven years young. We met a few years ago at church through the Fiancée at the time. Doris' husband, now deceased, was a bonafide World War II hero. Her favorite place to eat in Poughkeepsie is (you guessed it!) the Cracker Barrel, and her favorite thing on the menu is (you guessed it, again!) the catfish plate.

Believe it or not, Doris is my secret weapon on this walk.

Now and again, I'll call Doris now from the road. She's got this giant hardbound atlas next to the easy chair in her living room, and whenever I call, she'll ask me where I am today. Burns, Oregon; Nampa, Idaho; Valentine, Nebraska. I tell her the name of the nearest town and she looks it up in her big atlas. I can hear her licking her finger each time she turns a page. Then, when she finds it on the map, she tells me exactly where I am. "Oh, I see you," she will say into the phone. "There you are." That might sound silly and small, but when you're alone out here on the low road, that tiny sense of connection can really lift you up. We probably only spoke for a few minutes each time, but calling Doris was my favorite part of my day, by far. When I get back home, I will still probably call her so she can tell me where I am, and where I stand.

When this Doris comes back with coffee, I tell her the whole story, and she actually thinks it's pretty cool. At least, that's what she tells me. She takes our orders and walks back into the kitchen.

"She's not coming back," Jeff says when Doris is out of earshot. "She probably thinks you're a stalker."

"Really? I thought I explained it all pretty good: the walk, the atlas. Come on."

"We'll see." He slurps his coffee and looks out the window at the row of empty rocking chairs as they sway back and forth with the breeze. "I have a feeling my chicken-fried steak is getting tossed in the dumpster right now."

I'm pretty sure he's joking, but when Doris comes back with the manager a few minutes later, Jeff shoots me a look as if to say, *told you so.*

"This is Gerry, my manager," Doris says. Jeff is already standing up and putting his sunglasses back on his forehead, ready to leave. "I told him about your walk, and you two both being veterans, and he'd like to comp your meals today. On the house."

Jeff sits back down.

Gerry reaches out to shake my hand. "I think it's great, what you're doing. I saw you on the news last night. Good luck, and thanks for your service fellas."

Jeff mumbles from behind his coffee cup. "You're still a stalker."

After breakfast, we go back to Jeff's house and spread out all my new gear in his backyard. Then he shows me how to pack it all into my new ultralight backpack. He also rummages around in the garage and presents me with his old Leatherman utility tool. "Slip it on your belt, and never take it off. You'll probably use it every day." I strap on all my new gear, including my new hiking shoes I had sent to Jeff's house in the mail. Abby and the kids have just arrived from the visit from her parent's house, so they sit on the couch and judge the fashion show. I walk this way and that across the living room with my new gear. Maybe *sashay* is a better word.

"Work it," the oldest girl says.

Today, Jeff and Shayne have organized a walk with some other local vets from the Idaho Veterans Cemetery to a veterans' park in downtown Boise. It'll be nine-plus miles from the cemetery to the park, and from there I'll keep going on my own and end up at my old friend Baker's house on the eastern edge of town by the Interstate. I meet some great people on the walk today, including Shayne's mom and dad, who set up a kind of water station halfway into the walk, handing out cold bottles of water and energy bars from their trunk. It's mostly downhill for three hours, but when we get to the park Jeff is walking like his feet are on fire. "How many miles was that again?" he wheezes, sucking down water from his pack.

"About nine miles," I say, showing him the app on my phone.

"I don't know how you're doing this, every day," he says, flopping down on a rock.

I have to say, it felt good hearing about someone else's misery – okay, that didn't come out right. But only three weeks ago, you'll remember I was the guy who had to crawl on his belly to pee after walking 22 miles the first day. Now nine miles through downtown Boise feels like a warm-up for me, even with a bum ankle. It's frightening to think how quickly my body has adapted in such a short time. I've made it 400 miles in 22 days, which averages out to 18.2 miles per day; not quite the goal of 22 yet, but hey, this is a work in progress. So far, so good. I feel like tomorrow when I walk from Boise to Mountain Home it will be a fresh start, with all-new gear, and all-new enthusiasm. Hoo-rah.

I guess I'm looking for a second wind.

I've got another nine miles to go today, so I say my goodbyes to Jeff and Shayne and the rest of their motley crew. Tonight, I'll find Baker's house right as the sun goes down and we'll drink a few beers on his front porch while his wife Anna puts their kids to bed. Baker and I spent four years together in the MFA program at the University of Alabama, learning how to be writers and teachers. We're still learning on both, of course. Baker teaches writing here at Boise State, he loves it, and I'll bet he's got a cozy little office with a cozy chair just like mine back at Marist.

I tell Baker the story about Martone giving me an oar, but he still remembers it well. He's still got the book about kudzu, right here on the porch table. He says he always felt disappointed when word got around the campfire that Martone gave Zurhellen a real, live oar. It's good talking old times with my old friend, but it's getting late for me.

"Well, Zed, what's the biggest thing you've learned so far?"

Honestly, it takes me a long time to come up with an answer. You know me, normally I'd reply with some kind of snarky or self-effacing comment, but this time I don't. Maybe these two IPAs after a full day of walking are helping to put my guard down. Or maybe I'm just different person now after three-plus weeks on the road, who knows. After a deep breath, I finally give him my answer.

"You know what, Bake? I've learned that people are good."

I'll admit that kind of comes out of nowhere. But it's true: I've been relying on the kindness of strangers for three weeks now as I travel alone across America, and not once have I felt threatened or treated like some kind of outsider or pariah. I've only experienced the best of people, and so far, I've never seen the worst. When folks have stopped for me they've done it out of curiosity and kindness, not fear or prejudice. And that surprises me. It probably surprises you, too. The narrative we hear in America these days always seems to separate us: it's always red versus blue, black versus white, old versus young, us versus them. We're told that we probably all hate each other. But I'm here to tell you, I haven't seen any of that out here – not yet, anyway. And that is a very comforting thought.

Early the next morning, Baker and I tiptoe out of their creaky house before dawn, trying not to wake the kids. He drives me out to the last Boise exit on I-84, where Google maps assures me there's an access road that runs all the way along the interstate down to Mountain Home. It should be a perfect day. It's still dark when Baker pulls over below the underpass as the sparse traffic on I-84 rattles and hums above.

"All right, Bake. Thanks for everything."

He looks around at the scrub brush alongside the interstate. "You sure? I can stick around. At least until you make sure that access road really exists."

I'm already out of the car and sliding on my new pack. "It's got to be out there somewhere."

He turns around and drives off. As the sun peeks out I finally see what looks to be a dirt track, hidden among the sagebrush. Access road, my ass. This will be the first lie Google Maps tells me on this trip, but it definitely won't be the last. I count my blessings: at least there's something I can walk on. I take a hopeful selfie with the dawn, excited to break in my new gear. Today I'm hoping to find that second wind. I begin to follow the winding trail that hugs the interstate, but after a mile, it abruptly ends at a barbed wire fence. On the other side of the fence is a wide pasture, with a thick herd of cattle munching the abundant sawgrass and jimson weed. There's another wire fence on the other side of the field, about a quarter-mile away, but there's no sign of the trail starting up again, anywhere.

I'll stand there for a good fifteen minutes, cursing up a storm. Then I'll slide my pack off my shoulders and toss it over the barbed wire. Then I dip under the fence, retrieve the pack and keep walking. The pasture is lumpy and uneven, making the walking slow and precarious. I'm waiting for a rancher's pickup to come out of nowhere and run me down for trespassing, but there's not a soul out here that I can see. Except for the cows, of course, and so far they haven't seemed to mind the intrusion.

So much for that second wind.

I know I've talked a lot about taking the road less traveled in this book. Probably too much. Well, today I get to put my money where my mouth is. Today will be the day I find myself on a road *never* traveled, like Odysseus dragging his oar inland, looking for the way back home.

Day 23

MOUNTAIN HOME, IDAHO

ORIGINALLY, I dreamed up this whole VetZero Walk Across America thing as some kind of *Tommy Zurhellen Veterans of Foreign Wars Tour*. Just like Bob Hope, only on foot, hopping from VFW Post to VFW Post all the way across America, a humble Post Commander from Poughkeepsie depending upon the warm hospitality of his VFW comrades along the way. There are literally thousands of VFWs spread out across the country – at least, that's what it shows in the directory – so the odds were in my favor that I could line up a few dozen along the way. So before I started, I made sure to send letters and emails to my fellow Post Commanders at more than fifty Posts located near the route, in every town from Sandy, Oregon to Canandaigua, New York. I was excited to meet other veterans and hear their stories first-hand.

Here's the problem: none of them ever wrote back.

Well, I take that back. I did get one reply. It was an email in three words to be exact, from a Post Commander in rural Oregon. I had written him a while back that I'm walking across the country to raise awareness on veterans' issues and I'd be passing through their town, on a Monday. Was I expecting this guy to write back,

Strike up the band? Call the Mayor? Make Monday a local holiday?

No. But I wasn't expecting his reply, either: *We're closed Mondays*. That's the whole message.

I'm learning a lot of lessons on this walk, but today I'm learning to accept the one that makes me most sad: the VFW is dying. And I'm discovering this fact the hard way, as I walk through town after town where veteran service organizations like the VFW and American Legion once were a very, very big deal. For older generations, the Veterans of Foreign Wars was a central hub for just about everything in your hometown: holiday celebrations, concerts, town meetings, you name it. My aunts and uncles got married at the VFW, and yours probably did, too. But it's clear those days are gone, in most cases. The overwhelming majority of VFW Posts I pass on this walk are only an empty echo of their former great selves – if they're still standing at all. Sure, the building may still be there, and it might even say VFW on the sign outside, but I can tell you first-hand that most of the Posts I pass on this walk are empty. Some are open one day a week, and others don't open at all.

Now, I'm also happy to report that's not always the case. When we make it to Green River, Wyoming later in the book, trust me, we'll see vibrant VFW and American Legion posts working together in small town America, fighting the good fight to turn things around in their community. It's a whole lot of work, but they are doing it.

As for the reasons why these once-great veterans service organizations are fading to a lugubrious demise, I do have some ideas, but that's a completely different book. I will say in my three years so far as a VFW Post Commander, I've been to perhaps a couple dozen state meetings and they're all the same: twenty old white men with funny hats sitting at a dais up front for three hours, complaining about how they can't recruit younger veterans. They're not talking about how the young vets coming back from Iraq and Afghanistan have different needs and different perspectives than older vets who returned from Vietnam or Korea. Usually when I attend these meetings I sit in the back row and just shake my head as the old guard goes in circles up at the podium, talking about the same things over and over. I notice I'm not alone back here; I always see a few other young vets – younger than me anyway – sitting in the back, listening with their own disappointed frowns. When the old guys finally end the meeting, I notice these younger vets disappear almost as quickly and silently as they arrived. I have a feeling one day I'll attend a meeting and I'll be the young-est person in the whole room. That's the day I'll know the days of places like the VFW and American Legion are numbered.

If you're a VFW member reading this, you probably know exactly what I'm talking about. And it's a shame, because I actu-ally think an established organization like the Veterans of Foreign Wars can still could do a whole lot of good in the world. At my VFW Post in Poughkeepsie and many others around the world, I know we're certainly doing our best. But I also think the VFW has to change to attract these younger veterans who don't really care about having a place to drink cheap beer with their buddies or wearing funny hats. They want to have an opportunity to do meaningful service in their communities, in the middle of their busy lives. They want to feel like veterans.

The slow death of the VFW will be on my mind today on Day 23, as I reach the outskirts of Mountain Home on a sizzling afternoon. It's a desert town that's grown up around a huge Air Force base, so there won't be a problem crossing paths with veterans here. This morning was quite an off-road adventure, as I leapt barbed-wire fences and crisscrossed lumpy sorghum fields for hours until I finally located an actual paved road. Along the way, I actually uncovered an abandoned, weed-covered airstrip that I'm guessing must have been part of a training base during World War II. I definitely earned a cold drink or two. There's a gas station up ahead where I can find some shade and get out of this heat, for a spell. But a taxi cab pulls up alongside me on this two-lane blacktop and the young guy at the wheel gives me a nod. "Hey, you're the walker guy, right?"

This is how I meet Chris, a young USMC veteran who did multiple tours in Afghanistan and now is driving a cab in Mountain Home, where he grew up. My guess is he's around thirty years old, so he probably sees a wobbly guy like me with my white beard and VFW hat as some kind of fossil. He offers to drop me off at the gas station up ahead at the crossroads, and I accept, since I'm just about out of gas. We talk for a few minutes about the walk before he speeds away in his cab to finish his shift, before he heads over to his night job, tending bar at a local watering hole. It's a quick, refreshing conversation with a younger vet who seems passionate about helping other vets in his community. I wish I had more of them out here, and I wish we had more young veterans like Chris.

An hour or so later, as I'm walking the last couple of miles into Mountain Home proper to look for a supermarket and a cheap motel, a minivan pulls up alongside me and screeches to a halt, the door sliding open before the vehicle has even stopped. For a split-second, I'm thinking this is some kind of kidnapping plot. Okay, maybe a split, split-second. There's a college-age girl in sunglasses riding shotgun and when she leans out the window, I can see three more people behind her, including the driver.

"It's you!" the girl shouts like we're old friends at a high school reunion. "We've been waiting for you, dear. Hop in." She gestures to the open door behind her.

I'm a little speechless, and a little nervous. And did she just call me *dear*? "Chris sent us," she says, handing me a business card for the taxi service. "I work there, too. He told us about a veteran walking across the country, and we had to come out and meet you. We'll drive you anywhere in town you need to go," she says proudly. "Your chariot awaits."

I'm flattered, but I tell her I've already accepted one ride today from Chris, so I'll need to finish the day under my own power to reach my goal of 22 miles. This answer seems reasonable to her, and she nods. "Far out," she says. "Call us if you need anything, anything at all, okay?"

"What you're doing is awesome," somebody else yells from the minivan.

"Yeah," the girl says. "What she said."

"Thank you," I say. They hand over a few bottles of cold water that they've brought, and I ask them to show me the way to the nearest grocery store. I thank them again, and just as fast as it arrived, the van does a sharp, screechy U-turn in traffic and hauls ass towards downtown.

Now I know how Elvis felt the first time he visited Vegas.

After a few more blocks, I find the supermarket and grab some dinner to stuff in my pack. Now all I need is a place to sleep tonight. All the mom and pop motels are packed into a stretch of the town's main drag, another mile or two away. I check the day's mileage on my phone and I'm right on target: 20.9 miles walked today, so far. One more mile until I can collapse onto a creaky motel bed, eat, and watch some TV until I fall asleep. I've also got to bust out the First Aid kit and put some antibiotic ointment on all these scratches and cuts I have on my hands and legs from climbing barbed-wire fences all morning.

I've just about reached the motel mile when a blue Ford pickup rattles up to me and stops as I'm passing a gas station. This time, a woman in her thirties gets out. She's got a grey Pitbull riding shotgun, and it sticks his head out the window curiously, snuffing at me a bit. "Been looking for you," the woman says, holding her hand out to shake. "You're the walker guy, am I right?"

I nod, although I'm starting to feel like I'm on a merry-go-round.

"Chris put together a collection for you, and we raised enough to get you a room at the Marriott, out by the Interstate. It's nice. Trust me, you don't want to stay at any of these," she says, jerking her thumb at the seedy-looking motels ahead.

"I'm beginning to think Chris runs this town," I say. She smiles.

"You know what, you might be right."

Later, Chris drops by my swanky room at the Marriott with a wad of cash to donate to VetZero. "I took up another collection at the bar," he says with a smile. "In Mountain Home, veterans are loved as well as respected."

"I can see that," I say. We talk some more, and he clues me in on his service in the Marine Corps and the mental health challenges he's faced, including suicidal thoughts and depression. "That's why your cause is near to my heart."

Yes, the VFW as we know it is dying, but young vets like Chris are starting to form their own service organizations, usually through social media and shared interests, like motorcycles and sports. They're doing their own thing, much like the veterans returning from the Spanish-American War way back in 1899 did, forming the original Veterans of Foreign Wars. Now, I don't like the fact that Chris and so many other young vets like him view traditional veteran service organizations like the VFW and American Legion as outdated, obsolete, elitist, and out of touch. But I do understand why. And I realize the VFW and Legion aren't going to last much longer unless they begin to understand how our younger veterans from Iraq and Afghanistan are different than previous generations of vets. It's going to take more than lip service, or coming up with a new logo or catchphrase to attract these young heroes; it's going to take humility and dialogue. I'm worried the old timers will never show interest in either of those traits. I guess time will tell.

Day 31

BURLEY, IDAHO

I 'M WALKING down a sidewalk in a sleepy little village called Burley, Idaho around noon when a motorcycle rumbles past me on the main drag into town. It's loud, but I must be completely lost in my own mind again – damn you, Baby Shark song! – because as soon as the bike passes me, it almost causes a five-car accident making an abrupt U-turn right in the middle of the busy street, before rolling onto the sidewalk right in front of me. It's a beautiful old Harley custom rat bike, and the guy in the saddle is just as striking: with his bushy white beard, do-rag and anchor tatts, he looks like a cross between Santa Claus and some kind of sea monster. I want to shout, "Release the Christmas Kraken!" when he finally kills the engine, but let's face it, I don't need any new enemies out here on the low road. Especially new enemies riding bad-ass bikes who look like they just got back from Davy Jones' locker.

"Name's Bob," he says, kicking out the stand. "Are you that walker fella?"

I nod. I should be used to being stopped by now, but it's still a surprise each time. "I turned around in traffic just to meet you," he says in a deadpan stare. "So this better be worth it." Bob turns out to be a Vietnam vet, a Navy man; he was an Airedale (flight deck crew) stationed on the USS Kitty Hawk back in the late 60s and early 70s. His – ahem – dry sense of humor actually reminds me of my own Uncle Bob, who's also a Vietnam vet (and whom we'll actually see later in this book, when I get to Michigan!)

Bob folds his arms and sits square on his bike like some kind of bearded Buddha. "Are you really walking all the way to Poughkeepsie?"

I nod again, but this time I can't stop from grinning, ear-to-ear. He cocks his head. "What's so funny?"

"You're the first person out here to pronounce *Poughkeepsie* correctly."

"Is that a fact," Bob says. "Do I get a chicken dinner?"

I don't have a prize on me, so I compliment his ride instead. It's a 1990 Harley soft tail, chromed out with those super-loud Vance Hines pipes to scare the neighbors. With one look, I can tell someone has done a ton of work on it – definitely a labor of love.

I'm taking a closer look at the scrollwork when Bob tells me a story I won't soon forget. The bike used to belong to his best buddy Red, who was also a Vietnam vet. They had grown up in this small Idaho town together, and they joined the Navy together in the late 60s, but Red had passed away a few years ago and the bike fell to Bob. And he tells me he rides it every chance he gets. "Makes me think he's still riding with me," Bob says. I don't have the heart to ask how Red died, and I'm not going to speculate. I'm just grateful Bob trusts me enough to share his story. But I can tell he misses his buddy something awful, though. "What are you going to do," Bob says in a wheezy sigh. "Everyone's got to go sometime, I guess."

We talk for another twenty minutes or so as the midday traffic whizzes past on the town's main thoroughfare, two old sailors comparing sea stories. When he notices the VFW logo on my ragged shirt, we get into a conversation about the younger vets coming back from Iraq and Afghanistan, and how these veterans don't see much value in a place like the local VFW or American Legion. Bob's a member of the VFW Post here in Burley, but it's closed most of the time.

"It's about fellowship," Bob says. "They don't think they need it, but they do."

We shake hands and Bob punches his Harley back to life. "Okay," he shouts over the exhaust noise. "I guess it was worth it." And then he speeds away into traffic, leaving me there on the sidewalk alone.

As the word slowly gets out about the VetZero Walk Across America, more and more folks are stopping me on the road. Most are veterans, some aren't. Most want to share their story, some don't. You might think it could get old, getting stopped all the time while walking, but I'm happy to report it's actually the opposite: every day out here, I'm looking forward to meeting someone new. Each morning I wake up eager to hear new stories from veterans living all across America, veterans like Bob and Windhorse. And I feel so honored that these amazing veterans trust me enough to share their secrets with a big guy in a funny hat.

Day 34

McCAMMON, IDAHO

B ACK IN Portland on the first day, my old shipmate Paul and I made a side bet while we walked. We called our bet *First Blood Day*. We're both enormous fans of the 1982 movie *First Blood* where Sly Stallone plays Vietnam veteran John Rambo, and Brian Dennehy plays Will Teasle, the sheriff of a small Northwest town that Rambo is walking through. Teasle immediately looks at the homeless veteran as an unwanted nuisance and escorts Rambo to the other side of town, hoping he's seen the last of this mangy drifter. But when Rambo returns to eat at the local diner, the sheriff arrests him for vagrancy, and his deputies abuse him in the town jail. "All I wanted was something to eat," Rambo says later in the film, after he's wreaked havoc as revenge, in true Hollywood fashion. Sure, it's not the greatest movie ever made, but I can almost guarantee the veterans in your life have all watched it a dozen times (especially the Vietnam vets, who actually received this horrible treatment and much worse when they returned home, fifty years ago) because the movie exposes an old stereotype America still harbors today about its homeless veterans: there must be something wrong with them. If they are homeless, we're told, they're probably dangerous. And if they have mental health issues, well, they probably brought those problems upon themselves through substance abuse, bad life choices, and so on.

You know exactly what I'm talking about. Yes, we do a great job in America *talking* about how we support veterans, and our homeless in general – especially around election time. But when it comes to truly confronting the problems our veterans face each day, let's admit it, as a nation we have not walked the walk. We have put our heads in the sand. We have passed the buck, and we pass the blame to the VA or politicians or nonprofits like the VFW. We don't want to do the work to make things better. We don't want to hear how difficult it is for veterans to transition back to civilian life, or how easy it becomes for veterans-in-crisis to consider suicide. We don't want to hear the truth, because that would mean we'd have to admit our failure to protect the men and women who have protected our country. We always say, *thank you for your service*, but deep inside we know that hollow saying does absolutely nothing to help a veteran. It doesn't connect veterans with the mental health resources they need. It doesn't put food on their table when they lose their job. No, saying *thank you for your service* only helps us feel better about doing nothing. It assuages our guilt. It allows us to feel morally superior, as if we're nothing like the character of Will Teasle in *First Blood*, because at least we can say that we care.

Now, let me be clear: neither Paul nor I anticipated, even for a second, that I'd witness anything close to the vicious treatment Rambo received while I was on my own walkabout across America. Obviously, there's a huge difference between Hollywood and real life. But nevertheless, the *First Blood Day* wager I made with Paul on that first day was simple: how many days into the walk would it be until I'm stopped by local law enforcement, just for being a stranger in a strange land? I remember Paul believing it would happen very quickly, maybe by the end of the first week, and I thought it would happen a little farther down the trail, during the third or fourth week (Paul, feel free to correct me on the details, shipmate, if you're still reading.)

Either way, the winning entry would officially turn out to be today, Day 34, about a mile outside a tiny town called McCammon, Idaho, when I'm stopped by a Bannock County Sheriff's deputy on my way into town.

Here's the story.

Today's trek has been a long one: twenty-four miles from Pocatello to McCammon, along the scenic edge of Indian Rocks State Park. I'm really tired and ready to get off my feet, but I also feel lucky, since I've been able to reserve a room in the one hotel in the tiny hamlet of McCammon. It's getting close to sundown when I finally see a little brown sign up ahead that reads *Welcome to McCammon, Population 809*. My phone says I've got less than a mile to the hotel if I follow this road straight through town. I can't wait to put a fork in this chilly day by crawling into my room, crawling into the bed, and collapsing there for the rest of the night – before I have to get up and do it all over again when the funeral gong on my phone rings at six in the morning.

I'm close to the McCammon sign when I hear tires crunching the gravel on the soft shoulder behind me. I stop and turn around to see a sheriff's cruiser behind me; there's a young guy in wraparound shades and a tactical vest sitting behind the wheel. It feels like hours before he even looks up at me as I stand there patiently; after a while, he holds up his finger like a school teacher, signaling me to wait. I'm not nervous, just annoyed that I'm not in a warm bed right now. I figure he's looking down at his computer screen and calling back to headquarters — probably checking for any APBs for a six-foot-six drifter who looks like Grizzly Adams. Walking stick. Smells like piss and roadkill.

Finally, the deputy opens his door and steps out. "Hi there," he says from behind the driver's door. I notice one hand is resting up on the roof of the vehicle, and the other hand is hooked into his utility belt in front of his weapon. "How are we doing today, sir?"

Okay, young Padawan, this isn't my first space rodeo. I'm old enough to know that when a peace officer says, "How are *we* doing," using that royal we, then he or she is not asking how you are doing, friend. Instead, he or she is really trying to find out what you're doing here. The question really is, "Do you belong here?"

Of course, the answer is always no.

"We're doing great," I reply with some false cheer. "Can I help you?"

"I was going to ask you the same thing," the deputy says. "Where you headed?"

Of course, the grumpy old veteran part of me wants to tell him, *none of your damn business.* But I take a deep breath instead; I realize I'm the stranger in a strange land here; I'm the homeless veteran traveling alone, far from home. "I'm headed right here, officer," I say, pointing to the McCammon sign. "I'm staying at the hotel in town."

"Is that right," he says. "Which hotel is that?"

I smile and tell him the name. "Only one hotel around here, far as I can tell."

"That's the one," he says approvingly, like I just passed the first section of an exam with a dozen sections to go. "And you're just out here ... walking?"

I give him the boiler plate: I'm a veteran walking across America from Portland, Oregon back home to Poughkeepsie, New York to raise awareness on veteran suicide and veteran homelessness in our country. When I say this, his body language immediately shifts from suspicion to relief. "I think I saw you on the TV," he says now, like we're old friends who didn't recognize each other at first. "That's great."

What this young deputy doesn't know is, behind my calm smile I'm a little angry. I'm not angry that he stopped me; I've been stopped by law enforcement on this walk more times than I can count, and I'll be stopped plenty more times before I make it all the way home. But this is the first time I've been stopped and automatically treated like an outsider, a drifter, a *person of interest*. What if this young guy hadn't seen me on television? What if I was just any homeless veteran, and not the one who happens to be trekking across the country? And what if I was a person of color, or a woman, walking alone on this lonely road in Idaho? I'd like to think the encounter would have gone exactly the same – after all, that's the America I want to live in, and I know that's the America you want to live in, too. But honestly, it would be naïve for us to think so. Getting stopped today is nothing more than a nuisance for me personally; I'm a big, middle-aged white guy. But it reminds me that for so many Americans, and many others who come to America in search of a better life, that simple police stop can become so much more, in terms of life or death.

Honestly, the first draft of this chapter on Day 34 was a lot longer. Originally, I felt this encounter with this young deputy would be a good opportunity for me to springboard into some broader topics and issues important to our bigger discussion about Broken America – a real discussion about institutional racism, social justice, police brutality, white privilege, you name it. It was going to be a chance to elevate this book about a guy walking across the country into a real, live *memoir*. I wrote the first couple paragraphs of this chapter shortly after

I returned home in 2019, using the notes in my journal to recreate the story.

But between the end of my walk and the beginnings of this book, 2020 happened. Obviously, I realize there's a much larger conversation that needs to happen in America about all these things, but that conversation may be too large and complex for a memoir about a big privileged white guy in a funny hat, walking across America. I'm thankful that conversation finally begins in earnest in 2020, but only after the heartbreaking losses of Americans like George Floyd, Breonna Taylor, and many others. I feel like any attempt in these pages to speak on these issues would only seem hollow; you've probably already noticed I'm trying very hard not to hit any political buttons in this book, even though I'm writing *The Low Road* during the one year it seems impossible to escape the melee of charged political discourse. I don't have to tell you that 2020 has provided a critical education for all of us, in so many ways. If you're reading this book in 2021 or beyond, you've made it through the toughest of years, and you probably have the scars to prove it. You don't need me telling you about it, all over again. I will say, however, that we need to listen to the voices of people in America – particularly our younger voices – who are trying to get our attention on the things that really matter to them. Even if it's disturbing. (Check that: *especially* if it's disturbing.) Sometimes we have to walk a mile in someone else's shoes to really understand what they're going through. All I wish for 2021 is for all Americans to wonder, *do you belong here?* a little less when they see a stranger, and start asking, *how can I help?* a little more.

The young deputy asks me if I want a lift into town before he gets back in his vehicle, but I politely decline. I stand there watching his shiny black-and-white Bannock County Sheriff's cruiser make a U-turn in the empty road and motor away into the distance.

Day 39

BEAR LAKE, UTAH

Today I'm walking Highway 89 along the western shore of picturesque Bear Lake in Utah. I'm told they film a lot of car commercials here, and I can see why: the shimmering azure blue of the lake and the snow-capped mountains in the distance serve as an impressive backdrop. But today, I don't think anyone's filming because currently it's a frigid 31 degrees that feels downright subzero with a constant wall of wet, sloppy snow blowing nonstop into my face. I'm completely drenched and chilled down to the bone but I've still got eleven more miles to go before I reach a little town called Fish Haven and a rental cabin that's allegedly waiting for me. My glasses are completely iced over but I can see well enough to spot a billboard up ahead that says *WELCOME TO BEAR LAKE – THE CARIBBEAN OF THE ROCKIES.* Below the words they've got a sunny beach with a couple kids in floaties running around in the sand. But right now my lips are turning blue and my soggy feet feel like two blocks of ice -- so this does not remind me of the Caribbean.

The billboard gives me a good chuckle but soon after I pass it, a Bear Lake Sherriff's pickup cruises slowly past me and stops on the shoulder about fifty yards ahead. Immediately I have a flashback to that young cop back in McCammon and I think, *here we go again*. The red and blue lights on the truck go on. A stocky guy in camouflage gear, tactical vest, buzz cut and wraparound shades hops out. His name patch on his vest simply says *Carlos*.

"Hey," he says, ambling up to me. "Did you just eat at the Subway back there?"

Indeed I did. About two hours ago I was on a back road when a Toyota 4Runner pulled up alongside me with a gigantic hound dog rubbernecking its massive head out the backseat window. The woman driving rolled down her window. "Are you the walker guy, the veteran? I saw you on TV last night!" Her name was Sarah. She said she recognized the funny hat. We talked for a few minutes, mostly about all the veterans in her extended family, and then she asked if I was planning on stopping in the next town for lunch. "They've got a Subway up there in Paris, not much else." I said that sounded perfect; I was starting to get pretty hungry.

When I got to the tiny hamlet of Paris, I stopped into the Subway and at the counter there's a $20 gift card waiting for me, courtesy of Sarah.

Chalk another one up for the kindness of strangers.

"News travels fast around here," Carlos says. He's an Air Force veteran who moved out here from Texas about five years ago. He's got his young son in the backseat of the truck. "I want you to meet him." We walk back to the truck and I meet his eight-year old kid. "Hey *hijo*, this man is walking across the whole country by himself."

"Why?"

"Because I'm out of my mind," I say. The kid seems satisfied with that.

Carlos notices I'm shivering so he reaches out to feel the thin fabric on the sleeve of my drenched VFW jacket. "This is all you got?" When I say yes, he shakes his head in disbelief and lets out a whistle. He turns around and points to the misty mountains looming across the lake. "You see that? That's *Wyoming*," Carlos tells me, and when he says Wyoming with a heavy sense of doom in his voice, he might as well be saying Mordor. "If you think this weather is bad, let me tell you, Wyoming will kill you. You'll get a foot of snow one day, and then a hundred degree heat the next."

I tell Carlos I've been in touch on Facebook with another veteran who's trying to walk across America this summer; a few days ago, the guy told me he'd decided to leapfrog Wyoming and start again in Nebraska. At the time, I couldn't understand why. Now it makes sense.

"One thing's for sure," Carlos says, tugging my wet sleeve again. "That jacket ain't getting you through Wyoming." He thinks for a bit. "But I tell you what, hold on a minute." He grabs the radio on his vest and calls into headquarters. "Meet me out here on 89," he barks into the mic. "Bring the search and rescue truck." It takes me a moment to realize I'm the one being rescued. "We've got some foul weather gear stashed in the truck. Maybe there's something big enough to fit you."

Sure enough, a few minutes later another Bear Lake Sheriff's truck pulls up on the shoulder behind us. Now the cars pass by extra slow, rubbernecking to see why *two* units have stopped for this big guy in a funny hat. They must think I am a very dangerous man. The second deputy is a lot younger than Carlos but no less helpful. They open up the workbox in the back of the big truck and rummage around for a while until Carlos presents me with a waterproof hooded jacket and a balaclava. "These should help," he says. I put them both on right there on the spot. The jacket fits perfectly, and I feel better already -- good enough to take on the entire state of Wyoming, though? We'll see about that.

Tonight I will sleep in a caretaker's cabin next to a cemetery in the next town over. There's no plumbing but there's some old paperbacks on a shelf next to the wood stove, so I'll re-read *The Hobbit* for about the hundredth time, to help me fall asleep. I'm resigned to another dinner of energy bars and Chips Ahoy but right around sundown, a nice couple who live down the road knock on the cabin door, carrying a fantastic turkey dinner with all the trimmings. "Word gets around fast here," the guy says. "We really love what you're doing." I'll eat enough for three people, grateful again for the kindness of complete strangers. And right before bed, I'll make a quick call to Doris back in Poughkeepsie so she can find Bear Lake on her giant coffee-table atlas, and tell me where I am. She'll tell me it sounds like I'm coming down with something. She says she can hear it in my voice.

"Bear Lake, okay," she will say, finding it on the Utah page. "There you are."

"People out here call it the Caribbean of the Rockies," I say, shivering.

"Oh, honey," she says. "People are lying to you."

KEMMERER, WYOMING

Y ESTERDAY ON Day 42, I woke up at dawn on Rendezvous
Beach on the southern tip of Bear Lake with an inch of snow
covering my tent. Caribbean of the Rockies, indeed. A couple of
hours later, it's still only a few ticks above freezing when I get
caught up in a massive traffic jam on Highway 30 as I close in
on the Wyoming border. But this traffic jam isn't made of cars or
RVs – no, it's a sheep drive. Yes, you read that right. Five or six
ranch hands on horseback and ATVs are slowly coaxing a stubborn
herd of about a thousand sheep (this is a guess) out of their lamb-
ing pens and up to the pastures on top of the ridge. "It's that time
of the year," one of the pokes on horseback tells me. The problem
for everyone else on Highway 30 is, there's only one road to get
there, no matter if you are a sheep or a human. There's already a
line of cars waiting patiently at the crossroads when I get there;
we all watch as wave after wave of ewes and their lambs meander
up the winding highway. There are a lot of strays running this way
and that; I notice the ewes will chase their lambs when they stray
too far, bleating up a storm, adding to the general chaos. I take a
load off and hunker down on a wood bench in front of a Sinclair
station, taking it all in, munching on peanut brittle as I wait. After

a good half-hour, though, I begin to realize this slow-motion stampede is going to take all day – bad news for a guy who has to walk 42 miles over the next two days to reach the town of Kemmerer, Wyoming and get his next mail drop. So I finish my makeshift meal, grab my walking stick and join the ranch hands, eager to see how good a shepherd I might have become if my life choices had turned out differently.

"Yee-haw!" I shout, tapping the bottom of my stick against the pavement as I walk along the highway. Not too bad, I think; the sheep seem to be listening. Some of them, at least. It's pretty clear my *yee-haw* definitely needs some work, however. I get in as much practice as I can for the next couple miles, until the herd finally veers off the steep highway and onto their grassy pasture. I bid the real shepherds farewell and continue my climb up the two-lane highway. There's not much out here other than endless tufts of sagebrush and a few jackrabbits.

Tonight, I'll rely on the kindness of strangers yet again, when a young couple named Josiah and Melody take me in; they run a working ranch right on the edge of the Utah-Wyoming border. It's a real ranch, all right; Melody asks if I want to watch them brand some cattle, but I fall asleep before the action begins. They let me crash in one of the many cabins on their property and even supply me with a giant breakfast in the morning in their kitchen, before the whole family heads off to church. Their two small children, a boy and a girl, have about a kazillion questions for the big guy in a funny hat who is sitting next to them at the kitchen table, as we all chow down on a towering pile of pancakes, eggs and sausage together.

"Why do you have that stick?" the girl asks.

"It's good for bears," I say. "Oh, and sheep, too." I make a big deal out of telling them my shepherding story from the day before. At least, I use a lot of hand gestures. I figure they'll be impressed with my newfound herding skills.

"Yee-haw?" the little boy says with a sour face. Both kids laugh. "That's not what you say to a *sheep*. That's what you say to a *cow*."

"*Duh*," the girl says. "Where do you come from?"

"Poughkeepsie," I say, but to them it might as well be Mars. "It's in New York."

After breakfast, Josiah gives me a quick ride back out to the highway, so I can pick up where I left off the night before. He tells me they'll have the congregation say a prayer for me at church. I tell him I can use all the help I can get. Josiah also lets me know I'll be passing by Fossil Butte National Monument on Highway 30, about halfway between here and Kemmerer, and it's definitely worth a look.

"You got a great place out here," I say to him. "You should be proud."

He nods. "Thanks. If we can just find a way to market sagebrush, we'll be rich."

Today is Day 43! I'm excited to start a brand-new state – hello, wild Wyoming! – but I'm even more excited because I have mail waiting for me at the local post office, if I can get there before it closes. This will be my third mail drop of the walk; so far, I've asked folks on Facebook to send me a postcard or a snack when I've passed through Burns, Oregon and then again in Nampa, Idaho. I mentioned my favorite snack of all time are Nutter Butters, and that's pretty much been the bulk of it, a few packs here and there. Overall, the response has been pretty good, and I've been very grateful for the love and extra calories both times.

I make it to the post office in Kemmerer with twenty minutes to spare until the counter closes for the day. It's only a tiny plywood shack tucked away on a side street by the railroad tracks. The front area is so cramped, I have to turn sideways to get the door to close behind me. There's a woman with greying hair and horn-rimmed glasses behind the counter. As far as I can see, it's a one-woman operation; there not much room for anyone else back there, anyway. The back wall is stacked almost to the drop ceiling with packages.

"Afternoon," she says sleepily. "Can I help you?"

"I hope so," I say with too much excitement as I fish around for my photo ID. "Do you have anything for Tom Zurhellen? General Delivery?"

The moment she hears the name, her eyes shut and her mouth twists into an angry snarl. She bows her head and lets out a long, tired breath. Then she slowly raises her arm and points right at my chest. "It's *you*." Then she stares up at me with a look of pure disgust, like I stole her car, or maybe her cat. Or both.

"See that?" she hisses, waving at the wall of packages. "All that is yours."

I look behind her at what must be at least three or four dozen boxes and bags. She must be joking. "Wait. All of it?"

She nods slowly. "Yes. All of it." Then from under the counter, she pulls out two thick stacks of letters and cards, strapped together with rubber bands. "These, too." When I tell her about the walk and explain why a tidal wave of packages had suddenly washed into her tiny post office, she softens a bit. "Honestly, I thought it was some kind of prank. I've been here twenty years, never seen anything like this before."

She's closing the window soon, so together, we haul everything out into the entry area in plastic bins and I lean on the windowsill for the next hour, opening parcel after parcel and consolidating all the items into individual piles: food pile, painkiller pile, sunblock pile, and ... uh, shall we say, the miscellaneous pile. The amount of stuff people sent me today on this mail drop is staggering, and very humbling. There's forty pounds of Nutter Butters here, alone. Yes, you read that correctly. I need a plan, and fast; somehow I have to find a good home for most of this stuff, because I sure as heck can't take it with me.

Ah, serendipity. The next person to walk into the post office to check his mailbox is a brawny, middle-aged guy named Mike. He has to navigate the stacks of junk food on the floor just to reach his box. "That your Jeep out front?" I ask him, and he nods with a quizzical stare. "Is there a senior center in this town? Or a veterans' home?"

"I work at the senior center," he says proudly. "It's about a mile down the road."

I don't even have to explain my plan to Mike before we form a two-man chain to heave bins full of Nutter Butters and everything else into the back of his ride. Then we drive the five blocks to the local senior center, where about a dozen residents are taking turns Wii Bowling on a big screen TV in the lunch room. I find the manager in her office and I say, "Do I have a story for you."

The residents are appreciative for the truckload of snacks and sweets, but they're much more interested in finding out more about the guy trying to walk across America. They want me to stay for dinner and maybe join them to roll a few frames on the Wii. It's good we're not playing for money because they are really, really good on this thing. They ask me a lot of questions about the walk, and why I'm doing it. They've never heard of Poughkeepsie, but they know it's a long walk to get there from here.

Day 48

GREEN RIVER, WYOMING

THERE WAS another veteran trying to walk across America this summer, taking pretty much the same route I am following right now. We've been able to swap a few messages on Facebook, keeping each other updated on our progress. (Yes, there was a bit of a rivalry going on.) This guy had a good month head-start on me when I got a message from him, proudly informing me he reached Wyoming. But a few days later, I get a brief, cryptic message from him: *Skipping Wyoming. Starting up again in Nebraska.* I don't know if he gave up altogether, or if he ever made it home. I never heard from him again. I don't know if he ever made it to the East Coast, but it sounds like Wyoming broke him.

Oh, Wyoming. I've only been here for a few days myself, and I can't blame him.

Two days ago when I passed a deserted campground called Weeping Rock, I reached the highest altitude I'll hit on this entire walk, about 8,300 feet above sea level. This is what Louis L'Amour would call the high lonesome. Back when I was planning the route for this summer, the thing that terrified me the most – more than the blisters, more than the bears, more than being out of water – was the altitude. Heck, I would run out of breath walking around

Poughkeepsie, which is about two feet above sea level, so crossing the mighty Rockies on foot was a scary proposition, to say the least. Altitude sickness became my nemesis before I even took my first step on the walk; I'd even have nightmares where I'd be floating up in space or underwater, close to passing out, unable to breathe. So to prepare, I'd spend way too much time tinkering on Google maps, trying to find the roads that kept me at the lowest possible altitude. I was so worried that early on in the planning process I decided to avoid Yellowstone altogether, even though that decision probably added 50 extra miles to the walk overall. Walking through Yellowstone would have been a highlight of the walk, but when I saw the 9,500-foot price tag, I looked for a less lofty alternate route. Which is why I'm probably the only human within fifty miles of Weeping Rock campground in central Wyoming, at the moment.

Now that I'm actually out here getting used to this thin Rocky Mountain air, most of the time I tell myself it's no big deal – *altitude shmaltitude, Wyoming! This is all you got? Bring it on!* – but then I'll hit a hill, even a little one, and I immediately start sucking wind like a fish that jumped out of the fishbowl. For some unknown reason I make the mistake of trying to do another sing-a-long request -- someone posted on the VetZero Facebook page they wanted to hear me sing Journey's feel-good anthem "Don't Stop Believin'" which is a great song, but it's probably the worst song choice when you can't breathe. But I give it my best shot.

Later when I find some cell service, I send Nora the sing-along video, along with a text that lets her know I'm still alive and breathing after attempting the death-defying stunt of trying to sing Journey at a whopping 8,300 feet. I know Evel Knievel would be proud. Not sure Steve Perry, the lead singer of Journey, would be so proud, however.

Ever cheerful, Nora texts back: *Wow! Hey, it's all downhill from here!*

I didn't think about it like that. She's got a point. I've made it to Day 46, and what do you know, it is indeed all downhill from here. That's a comforting thought.

When Nora posts the sing-along video, most of the comments have nothing to do with my singing. They're more like shouts of grave concern for my health. As in, Tommy sounds like he's about to pass out. Geez, is he all right? Can we send him oxygen at the next mail drop? If he does pass out, will we know where to send the authorities to fetch the body?

As you might expect, people have asked me a lot of questions about the walk. Most questions have been pretty normal, and others have been, well, less normal. But it's interesting to me that the two questions I get the most are (more or less) opposites. First, what's the most beautiful part of America you've walked through? And second, what's the most challenging part of America you've walked through?

For me, these two questions have the same exact answer. Wyoming!

I've lost a good thirty pounds since I've started this journey; my legs are toned like never before and my calves feel like iron. But it doesn't matter how in-shape you are, breathing is going to be a lot harder at seven or eight thousand feet above sea level. No wonder a lot of professional runners from all over the world do their road training in the air up here.

The things I hate most about Wyoming are the same things I absolutely love. Take the last three days, for example.

We forget that a lot of America is still wild. I know I forgot -- that is, until I had to walk across it, alone. We look at a map of the USA so often, we think we know it. But we don't. If you live in the city or suburbs, which is most of us, I think we've lost touch with the world around us. We take a lot of things for granted that, quite frankly, aren't written down on any map. In the city, everything is within reach. Transportation is easy. Shopping is easy. Talking on the phone or connecting to the internet are easy – and when that connection is down for whatever reason, even for a few minutes, we suddenly feel like the world is on pause. But what happens when you force yourself out of that bubble? What happens when you can't rely on all the comforts we've come to expect from living in our cities and towns across America?

Oh, baby, it's a wild world.

There's a whole different America out there that looks pretty much the same as it did a hundred years ago. I know, because I'm seeing it all at three miles per hour. From the high desert of Oregon all the way out here to the Medicine Bow mountain range in Wyoming where I'm walking right now, there is a wild world that runs on a different timeclock, and a different set of rules. And here's the thing: I've been out here so long that I'm actually getting used to it. I'm getting accustomed to the quiet and the loneliness. I'm getting used to not having a cell signal. The strange noises that once freaked me out walking out here alone – hello, mountain lions! – are just part of the scenery now. And when I get to a city or town, those noises are the strange ones now. Things have reversed, and it's only been a couple months or so out here on the low road, working things out on my own.

Listen, I grew up in the biggest city of all, New York, and the only place I would have seen antelope was at the Bronx Zoo. Out here, I am completely surrounded by antelope on a daily basis. They hiss at you if you get too close to the herd, and they don't run, they bounce – and when they do, it looks like they're flying on a magic carpet or something. I've seen other animals out here that I've only seen in books or nature shows, and this isn't some exotic African or Australian safari tour, this is one guy walking alone in Wyoming.

No sasquatch sightings to report yet, but hey, this walk is far from over.

These last three days between Kemmerer and Green River in Wyoming have been the wildest stretch of America that I will experience on the entire walk. When I left the town of Kemmerer three days ago, I walked east until I picked up a lonely highway called 372 as it runs parallel to the Green River as it meanders south. The highway is actually a couple miles distant from the river itself, so I made the executive decision to leave the pavement behind and walk along the riverbank itself. My Sawyer water filter can produce all the cold, clear water I can drink, and I've got plenty of food to last three days before I finally hit the town of Green River, sixty miles south.

I've also made fast friends with a fly fisherman named Carl, who's up from Denver to do some fishing on the Green River (and to get away from his wife and kids for a few days, I think.) Carl drives a beat-up Volkswagen van from the 1980s that needs prayers and a good push to get it started. He's following the river south at pretty much the same pace I am, scouting different fishing spots and trying to find river access roads from the highway, so we cross paths a lot out here the last three days. He even shared some of his whiskey supply with me on a chilly night on the first day we met, back at Weeping Rock campground.

So far on this adventure, I've seen plenty of wild spaces; the problem is, even though the wilderness is all around, I've still been stuck to the pavement. But for these last three days, I'm in heaven: I'm walking on the grassy bank of a twisty river all day, the way it probably looked hundreds of years ago. The only creatures I see are the birds, a few fish, and plenty of antelope that come down to the water to drink during the hot days. In the distance, I can hear the cars and trucks passing by on the highway a couple miles away. A few times, I've even thrown my shoes over my shoulder and walked barefoot in the shallows and sandy riverbank, the cold water and soft ground somehow breathing life back into my weary feet and toes. I don't speak to anyone save a couple of words to Carl here and there as our paths cross. The silence feels beautiful. I know when I reach the town of Green River I'm going to miss this solitude. Maybe the best part of these three days walking the river? I don't look at my phone, not once. There's no cell service out here anyway, but I don't even think to check. I am walking a river alone, with no traffic, no appointments, no conference calls, no conversations, and no distractions. And it's glorious.

I follow the lazy Green River for three full days of wild wonder until finally, it crosses I-80 and then make a left on the access road that runs alongside the Interstate. (Walking tip: pedestrians are forbidden on America's interstate highways.) As soon as I get close enough to hear the big rigs rumbling up and down the pavement ahead, my wilderness dream disappears into thin air. Suddenly I find myself back in civilization, my feet standing on pavement, the morning air smelling like diesel and dust.

Just as I reach the I-80 overpass, Carl passes me in the van, beeping the horn and waving out the window as he steers down the eastbound ramp, back towards Denver. I hope he's got enough prayers in him to make it all the way home. I know he's got no fish in the cooler to show his kids, but he's got a good story to take home instead. It's a tale of wild adventure that even Jack London would be proud to tell; it's about three days following a winding river with a big guy in a funny hat who's trying to find his way home.

I'm not expecting much from the town of Green River. I've walked through so many little towns that they've all kind of blurred together in my short-term memory: the names, the streets, the sights – pretty much everything except for the people. And as I reach the outskirts of Green River, Population 11,978, it looks like a lot of other sleepy towns that hug the interstate out here in the wild American West: lots of scattered singlewides, lots of plastic-roofed fast food joints, and lots of gas stations doubling as convenience stores, smoke shops, arcades, liquor stores, and whatever else you might need bad enough to escape the highway. So please forgive me when I say, I'm not expecting much out of the VFW in Green River, either. So far, I've passed by dozens of VFW and American Legion Posts on this walk, and most have been closed – some temporary, some permanent. And the few that were open for business weren't as excited as you may think to welcome a big guy in a funny hat trying to walk across America. Confused, more than excited. So I am figuring the VFW and Legion Posts here in Green River won't be any different.

About a week ago when I was freezing my butt off in Bear Lake, Utah, I got a message on Facebook from a woman here in Green River, asking if I was going to be walking near her town. She had been following the journey online and invited me to stop by the American Legion in Green River to meet some local veterans. I accepted and told her I would stop by the Post when I got into town, probably around sundown.

When I skirt around a big painted butte I can finally see the outskirts of Green River up ahead. After chugging up a final hill, I'm absolutely starving when I walk into town; I downed today's last energy bar a few miles ago. Luckily the first building I come across is a 50s themed diner, complete with the trifecta of Chubby Checker, Elvis and Fats Domino playing on endless repeat from the speakers outside.

Hello, Belgian waffles, triple side of bacon and chocolate shake!

I know there's another book to be written about how we often take our food for granted, but for now, it's safe to say I will always appreciate the value of a good meal after this walk is over. When I clean my plates and pay the check, the sun is starting to go down, so I check into the first mom & pop motel I pass, a two-story stucco joint called the Western. I check into my room to dump my back-pack, take a quick shower, and change my shirt (I only have two shirts with me.) The motel's not fancy, but hey, when you've just slept outside for the past four nights, well, any place with a bed and a roof is going to look like the Taj Mahal. Besides, the price is right. My phone has been off the last three days while I walked the river and got back to nature, so I turn it on and check all the messages I missed. The Fiancée has called a few thousand times, so I give her a call while I'm washing my grimy VFW shirt in the motel sink with a packet of shampoo.

"Where have you been?" she says as soon as she picks up. "I was worried."

"I was walking," I sigh as I fall back on the squeaky bed. "There was no cell service."

"For five days?" She puts me on speakerphone, and now I can hear her chopping something on a cutting board. "Where were you walking, the Moon?"

"Still in Wyoming. But, close." I rub my nose. "And it was three days, not five."

"Well, it felt like five." She keeps chopping as she catches me up on everything her kids are doing. She's making their lunches for school tomorrow, and they're at that age where a simple PBJ and bag of chips in a paper sack just ain't going to cut it. She's got a boy and a girl, both teens in high school, and there was time not very long ago when I felt like an actual full-time stepdad, doing the usual stepdad duties: rides to wherever, money for whatever, and showing up whenever to cheer like hell at an endless series of soccer games, dance recitals, school plays. I sat through *The Will Rogers Follies* three times and loved every minute of it. But things changed when their dad came back into the picture, about a year or so ago. Hey, I figure it was a good five-year run. At least I got to pretend for a while that I was somebody in their lives. Now the whole story feels like an open wound sometimes. I don't talk about it much, and I have no idea if being out here on the low road, so far away, makes that wound feel better or worse. Anyway, I get really sad when I have to think about it. Or write about it.

"Listen, I've decided," she says. "I'm going to come out and see you."

"Wow," I say, genuinely shocked. "Do you know where?"

"No clue. *Shit*," she says as she struggles to open a Tupperware container. "Okay, there we go. I know I've got the Habitat for Humanity trip with the kids coming up at the end of June, but I'm free after that for a few days until ... well, I can't remember exactly, but I've got something. I'll make it work. So, are you excited?"

"Very excited," I say. "Do you know when?"

"Nope. But I'll figure it out. I always do." She's finished making the lunches. "And I mean, you're not exactly going anywhere." There's a dramatic pause so I'm guessing she meant that as a joke. "Am I right?"

Okay, probably not a joke.

"Right." She has to get off to watch her daughter do a tap dance routine in the basement. I say, "I love you." Then I lie there on my back for a few more minutes, looking up at the ceiling. It's quiet, but I can hear a car pulling into the parking lot outside. If I don't leave soon I'll be late meeting Amanda and the crew at the local Legion Post, but I don't get up right away. I'm thinking over my latest conversation with the Fiancée, and how all our conversations these days seem like they're missing something. So I lie here for a bit and think about what I'm missing. I'm missing the part of the conversation where she asks me how I'm doing. I'm missing the moment where she yells something like, *you're a fucking Rockstar* when I tell her I just trekked three days in the wilderness alone. And I'm missing the part where she wants to listen to me ramble on about antelope or vultures or whatever else I met on the road today. I miss the part where she says I'm rooting for you, I believe in you. I miss the part where she says, "I love you, too."

I hang my shirt on the TV rack to dry, but I have to blow-dry my shorts because I'm wearing them down to the Legion post tonight. (Hey, if you're going to travel light, travel light.) At least I never have to ask *what to wear?* when I wake up in the morning.

The Tom Whitmore Post of the American Legion is only a half-mile or so from the motel, and downhill to boot, which is a perfect end to a long day because I know I'll surpass my daily goal of 22 miles by the time I walk back to fall asleep. The white stone building sits on a quiet side street, right off the main drag – which incidentally is called *Flaming Gorge Way*, definitely in the running for my favorite street name in the U.S.A. – and it's only a stone's throw from the massive switchyard that serves as the beating heart of this railroad town. The VFW is physically just around the corner, but as I'm soon to discover, the veterans in Green River all work together. As I walk through town I'm reminded of all the history buried in this part of the country. To a kid from the Bronx, this railroad town feels a lot like the Wild West I only got to read about in Steinbeck's brilliant road memoir *Travels with Charley*.

I step inside the Legion and I'm immediately surprised by a good-sized mob of folks who, for some reason, are here to meet me. Amanda introduces herself and her dad, who's a Vietnam vet and from what I can tell, also a bonafide local legend around these parts. Suddenly I find myself surrounded by a bunch of people who want to know everything about what I'm doing. I was expecting a few raised eyebrows, or maybe someone saying good luck, which is pretty much the normal response I've received as I pass by other VFW and Legion posts. But the folks here seem genuine and enthusiastic, and I have to say, it feels good. They present me with a generous donation check for VetZero, and we take a few pictures before I get to sit at the bar next to Amanda's dad as he holds court, telling some great stories about the history of this place.

I want to listen to him all night, but I have to get an early start for Rock Springs in the morning. Amanda shows me a great short-cut off the beaten path for tomorrow, that doesn't even show up on Google maps. "You start at the cemetery," she says, pointing up the hill. "There's an old dirt path that'll get you to Rock Springs."

Cemetery? Old dirt path? This sounds like an episode of *Scooby Doo.*

"Yeah, it's definitely the scenic route," she says. "But that's what you want, isn't it?"

By now, people on Facebook are asking if I have a morning routine, to get my body ready for each day walking eight or nine hours on the low road. Yes! It all starts with a good half-hour of intense moaning. Then I will sit up and press gently down on my puffy feet – left then right, left then right – like a woozy dance. If I stand on them right away, it will feel like I'm standing on a bed of needles. So I take it slow. When I feel strong enough to stand, I will take four Advil and a handful of joint compound pills before I start to actually walk around, loosening my knees, my hips, my ankles. Then comes the Vaseline. I try to buy the kind with aloe, because it smells a whole lot better, but I can't be choosy in the middle of nowhere. I will rub gobs of Vaseline under my arms, between my legs, on my nipples, on my heels, and in between my toes. Then I rub some CBD oil into my aching ankles. Then I'll wrap the tips of my second toes and pinky toes with athletic tape, before I slip on my thick hiking socks. The tape will help prevent blisters, but some days I get them anyway. Then I'll roll my ankles braces over my socks, and hopefully my feet are shrunk enough by now to slip easily into my shoes. Otherwise, there's plenty more moaning as I try to shove them in there. I can't bend my knees enough to tie my shoes, so I leave them tied. Almost ready. I slather on plenty of SPF 70 sunblock on my face and arms and especially my hands, since I have vitiligo which means there are parts of my skin that have no pigment. Finally, I roll some zinc onto my nose, whether it looks like a sunny day or not. Then I'm ready to drink some coffee, eat something, and get back out on the road.

All that takes about an hour, maybe a little more. Having a routine helps me find a rhythm to start each day. It gives me some measure of control, before I head out to face the unpredictable, unmapped world ahead.

Day 56

ALCOVA RESERVOIR, WYOMING

W E'VE ALL panicked at one time or another. But when you are walking alone in the desert and you run out of water, well, that's a special kind of panic. As a kid who grew up in a city, it hadn't really dawned on me until this walk that most of America is wild; you can't just walk around the neighborhood to find a faucet. As a younger man, I watched a lot of old movies, spaghetti Westerns mostly, where there's always some guy crawling on his hands and knees through a hot, hardscrabble desert under the scorching sun, half out of his mind with thirst. To be honest, whenever I watched that part I would always roll my eyes and mumble something like, *just suck it up, dude*. After all, didn't we all learn the same statistic back in fifth grade? The human body can survive three or four days without water.

Well, the nerd who came up with that statistic obviously never tried to walk across Wyoming in the summertime.

After today I can tell you first-hand: in the desert, it's more like three or four *hours* before your whole body starts to shrivel like a piece of dried fruit. You can actually sense body parts shutting down, one by one, when you're overheated and you run out of water. I feel like a human *Shrinky-Dink* out here, slowly broiling on a cookie sheet in the oven, if your memory of silly toys goes back that far.

When you are dehydrated, you get cramps in places you didn't know you could get cramps. Especially when you are big guy and you sweat as much as I do. Now it's true, I've run out of water before on this journey, but whenever I did, I always knew there was a gas station or a town coming up in the next few miles where I could drink my fill. And if there wasn't drinking water ahead, the worst-case scenario would be to pull out my trusty Sawyer water filter and fill an empty water bottle with water from just any water source. That actually happened a few times so far, the most recent a couple weeks back along the Green River – but even then, I wasn't really worried. I didn't panic, because I knew that in a pinch, the water filter would always save me.

So today when I reach an empty Black Beach Campground on the edge of the Alcova Reservoir with my water pack completely drained, I'm thirsty as hell, but I'm not really all that worried. I know I'll find a spot to set up camp and then draw all the water I need from the reservoir with my little Sawyer pump. But when I open my pack and look inside, a new feeling of terror slowly spreads over me: somehow I packed my gear too tight this morning, and the Sawyer pump is crushed into pieces. It's completely useless. I lick my cracked lips and look around the deserted campground for any cars or signs of life, but I don't see anyone. Slowly I start to feel the pain of that poor guy in the Western. Oh, I can see next week's headline in the local paper: NEW YORK MAN DIES OF THIRST AT RESERVOIR.

Like my man Samuel Taylor Coleridge wrote back in the day: *water, water everywhere, nor any drop to drink.*

I find some shade under a lean-to and try to figure out my options. Option A would be walking to a gas station the map says is about six miles further down the road, towards Casper. But that's roughly two more hours of walking when I'm already dehydrated. Option B would be to walk the mile back out to the main road and hope to flag down someone, but I just spent all day walking that same road, and it might be *more* than two hours before a car came by. And Option C would be to just drink unfiltered water from the reservoir, but getting sick from giardia and all the other zoomies living in lake water doesn't seem like a good plan, either. I guess I could go out to the main road and wait an hour to flag down the next vehicle that passes on the lonely highway.

Luckily for me, I spot a carload of college-aged guys on the other end of the reservoir, packing up from a day of swimming. I'm ready to drink the melted water at the bottom of their cooler when Tim comes up with a better idea. "There's a gas station about six or seven miles up the road, towards Casper. I could bring you back some big water bottles."

His two buddies squirm a little. I can tell they aren't too thrilled with wasting their time, coming back here to help an old homeless guy avoid dying of thirst.

"You're a lifesaver," I say to Tim, pulling some money out for the water.

"No need," Tim says. "Sit tight. We'll be right back."

Half of me doesn't expect to see these young guys again. But sure enough, after about a half-hour I see Tim's car coming back over the rise, kicking up dust on the access road. He hands me three big bottles of cold water, and I down one right there on the spot. "You were thirsty, all right," he says with a smile. I offer to pay again, but he just waves his hand. "Happy to help."

We talk for a few more minutes, and I ask him about his service. Turns out Tim was a member of the fabled 10th Mountain Division, and when he got out, he spent about three years on the streets as a homeless veteran himself, drifting around the country. When he got to Wyoming, he liked it so much out here, he decided to stay. And from the looks of it now, I'd say Tim is doing just fine.

That's a success story we need to see more often, especially for our younger veterans like Tim and so many like him, who are coming back from Iraq and Afghanistan without much support. We need to do better.

Thanks Tim, for looking out for a fellow veteran.

CASPER, WYOMING

I T's LATE afternoon on the day after I reach the Alcova Reservoir and right now, I'm closing in on the Casper city limits on Highway 220 when I see a black Tahoe barreling towards me, its fat tires suddenly screeching to a halt beside me. I'm not worried; I know who's driving before I even look up. "Hey, dummy," the guy behind the wheel says as he jerks the truck to a halt right beside me. "You walking out here all by yourself?"

This is my oldest Navy buddy T.C. We became fast friends on the very first day of bootcamp in Orlando, Florida and we've been long lost brothers, ever since. We both enlisted in the Navy right *after* graduating college, so that gave us some weird common ground right away. He's also one of only two people left in the world who still call me by my old nickname, Tellis, which has a story attached to it but not interesting enough to interrupt a chapter in this book. Anyway, I was supposed to be best man in T.C.'s wedding down in Orlando back in 1992 but I missed my flight and got to the church just as they were walking out. At least I was there for the reception, which took place at a beautiful beachside Ramada Inn down in Jupiter, Florida. I only remember the first half of that night, since I blacked out pretty much as soon as I went skinny dipping in the ocean. With somebody's sister. It may have been T.C.'s sister, I don't know.

I have been told the stories of what happened next, after the skinny dipping, but long ago T.C.'s mom made me promise never to share them. Safe to say, I don't think T.C. has ever forgiven me. Maybe that's why he was driving so damn fast towards me.

I dump my pack in the backseat and ease into the front, happy to be off my feet. "Okay, Tellis, first thing," he says as soon as I close the door. "You *stink.*"

I'm grinning ear to ear. "Thanks, buddy. I get that a lot."

I'm smiling at my old Navy friend because by now, that stink has become a sort of badge of honor for me. It's taken a couple of months of misery on the low road, but now, I'm finally starting to appreciate what it's really like to be a homeless veteran in America: the real sights, the real sounds, and of course, the real smells. Any magazine article can tell you what it's like for a veteran living on the streets today, but there's only way to show what those lives are truly like. Sure, I may smell bad, but I've *earned* that smell, just like I've earned the right to talk about being a homeless veteran because I've lived it. Honestly, I'm proud of it. I've earned every blister, every sprained ankle, every lost toenail, and yes, every layer of dirt and grime on my skin. You want personal hygiene, take the high road. But if you truly want to know how our 40,000 homeless veterans really feel on the streets of America, well, you've only got one option, folks.

You grin and bear it, and take your chances on the low road.

"I'm opening the windows," he says as he makes a quick U-turn back towards the Casper city limits. "You smell like beef jerky and piss."

"Aw, you love it. Reminds you of your Navy days."

"You got me there, Tellis." He tosses me a cold bottle of water he picked up from a gas station. "Still leaving the windows open, though."

After we got out of the service around the same time, T.C. and I lost touch for a while as our lives followed very different paths. He used his engineering degree from Virginia Tech along with his experience in the Navy to get a management position with General Electric, making turbines. T.C.'s a sharp guy and has the gift of gab, so from there, it didn't take long for him to reach the top of the food chain in the wind turbine industry, becoming a CEO for companies both here and abroad. We're the same age, and he's comfortably retired. Well, more or less. At least, he can find the free time to fly out to Casper, Wyoming to track down an old ship-mate walking along the road.

"It's good to see you, brother," I say, already finishing the liter of water. "Thanks for coming out here."

Now he's grinning, too. "Oh, there's nothing I'd rather do," he says. "Than getting lost in Wyoming looking for a guy who smells like beef jerky and piss." And just like that, it seems like old times. Suddenly, it feels like 1992 again, riding in T.C.'s maroon F-150 to hit the off-base strip clubs and seedy bars that clung to the old Orange Blossom Trail in Orlando. Veterans are a rare bunch: you might not see your shipmate or battle buddy for years and years after the service, but it usually only takes a few moments – or one wise-crack – to knock off the rust and bring you right back where you started.

Now, there's a super-power veterans have that other folks don't: time travel.

Sadly, there's no bars or strip clubs in our future here in Casper, though. We've actually got a tight schedule the next two days, with a couple of media interviews and meetings with both the Central Wyoming Counseling Center and the local chapter of the Vietnam Veterans Motorcycle Club. Oh, and in between all that, we've got to find a way to walk twenty miles or so, to keep on schedule.

"What did I sign up for," T.C. moans.

The Central Wyoming Counseling Center has generously

fronted me a room at a nice hotel in town. It's still early, so we decide to drop our gear off and walk the four or five miles across town to a coffee shop where I'll do my first interview with a reporter from the Oil City Press.

We're walking along a paved trail that hugs the north bank of the North Platte River, cutting right through the middle of the city. We're having a good time talking about the old times. About half-way to the coffee shop, we stop to take a few photos of a veterans' memorial wall that sits quietly along the walking trail. Up ahead on the trail, we see a runner rapidly approaching; it only takes a few seconds before he's already passing us at a pretty good clip. Abruptly, the guy stops in his tracks and turns back around, still running in place. He's looking at me with a suspicious eye, like he just saw my face on a wanted poster.

"Hey," he says, taking his earbuds out and pointing at me. "You're the guy."

Turns out, this guy saw me on the TV news a few days back. For me, this kind of encounter with folks on the road is becoming more and more common, but for T.C., who's been out here for a couple hours, a stranger recognizing me out of the blue like I'm some kind of celebrity is something very new. After a few minutes of quick conversation, the runner continues his flight down the trail and disappears around a bend. I start walking down the trail but T.C. is still standing there, his mouth wide open as if he's just realized today is the day he's walking across Casper, Wyoming with Brad Pitt or Jesus or the guy from those State Farm commercials.

In other words, he's giving me shit. I say, "Don't be so dramatic."

"Hey," he says, pointing at me just like the runner did. "You're the *guy*."

"Get used to it," I say, laughing out loud. "Pretty soon you're going to be picking the brown M&Ms out of the bowl in my dressing room, and you're going to like it."

"I didn't know you were the guy," he says, pausing to look back down the trail at the bend where the runner disappeared. "That was pretty cool."

We do the interview with the reporter from the Oil City Press over coffee, and T.C. might be talking more than I am about the walk and the reasons why I'm doing it – which is fine, because I'm happy not to warm over the same talking points I've been regurgitating for the last two months. Besides, T.C. is having a whale of a time, hamming it up as my unofficial press secretary.

After we finish the interview and thank the young reporter for coming out to meet us on a wet and windy day, T.C. and I walk down the street a couple blocks to a restaurant to meet Kevin and Bernice, who run the Central Wyoming Counseling Center here in Casper. They're actually from Poughkeepsie (small world!) and they've been following the walk since the start. The Central Wyoming Counseling Center deals with all sorts of mental health issues, including veterans' mental health, so they're really interested in the message we're trying to spread during the walk about raising awareness on veteran suicide and veteran homelessness in America. Tomorrow afternoon, I'll get a tour of their facility that sits on a bluff overlooking the city and meet some of their counseling staff.

As we wait to be seated, they ask about their old hometown. "I miss Poughkeepsie," Bernice says with an air of nostalgia.

I sit down gingerly in my chair and rub my aching knees. "Not as much as I miss Poughkeepsie." This is my first real meal of the day, not including the mixed nuts and little biscuits they leave in your hotel room, so I'm really hungry.

"Don't eat too much, guys," Kevin says. "We've all been invited for dinner tonight to our friend Sam's cabin. He lives up the mountain, outside Casper."

Bernice claps with excited. "Oh, you'll love him! He really is an eccentric veteran."

"Yeah, I've met a few on this trip," I say, nodding my head at T.C. across the table.

I end up ordering a salad.

"Guilty as charged," T.C. says, before ordering what seems like half the menu. He gives me a shrug. "What? All this walking makes me hungry."

After our late lunch, T.C. and I walk the five miles back to the hotel and somehow, we avoid being mobbed by more paparazzi on the trail. T.C. is very sad about this, but he more than makes up for it by pointing at me whenever we're around other people – at a street corner, in the hotel lobby, in the hallway – and saying, "Hey! You're the guy!"

At first I'm embarrassed, but after the first dozen times, I practice my Pope-wave and red carpet walking skills. Hey, if you can't beat 'em, join 'em I guess.

We have just enough time to shower and make a couple phone calls to the folks we love before Kevin and Bernice pick us up in the lobby to take us up the mountain to Sam's house. Honestly, I'm not super-excited for this dinner with strangers. I'd much rather be alone and spend my time sleeping, than using up my energy talking with new folks. But by the time we pull up to Sam's cabin, I'm feeling better. Part of that has to do with Kevin and Bernice: they have so much energy, it's hard to be sullen. The other part is, Bernice has made a pan of her world-famous macaroni and cheese, and it fills the car with the most heavenly scent. T.C. and I are cramped into the backseat and secretly I think we're both half-hoping to get into an accident, just so we can "save" Bernice's mac n' cheese from being destroyed in the wreck. Yeah, it smells that good.

Sam's cabin is even more remote than advertised. It's is hidden behind the tree line at the end of a gravel path that snakes up Casper Mountain and passes Bear Trap County Park (yes, we're worried) before stopping abruptly at a boulder. The cabin sits hidden on top of the boulder, and I can tell right away it's been a labor of love for the guy who built it. Suddenly I'm reminded of Windhorse's mountain retreat, back in the high desert of Oregon.

Masa tells me the story of his battle buddy Ricky, who died in a chopper crash when they were deployed to Iraq in 2008. Then he holds up his wrist to show me the silver bracelet on his wrist. "I had this made when I got back stateside," he says. "It's got Ricky's name engraved on the inside. That was twelve years ago. I haven't taken it off since."

"I can vouch for that," his wife says, with a warm smile.

"It's beautiful," I say, because it's true. I take a closer look at the inscription.

"Thank you," Masa says. He takes a deep breath. "I'd like to ask you a favor. I'd like you to wear it for the rest of your walk. I'd like you and Ricky to see America together, see everything. I think he'd like that."

At this point, there's not a dry eye in the house. Even T.C. is silent. And I have to admit, I'm pretty choked up myself, barely able to speak. "It's going to be an honor," I manage to say. Masa slips the bracelet off his wrist and hands it to me. I put it on, thanking him again. Masa smiles proudly. I promise him I won't take it off until I could return it to him in person, after the walk was over. That seems like a tall order; after all, I've still got around 1,700 miles left to go, and who knows when I will be able to get back to Casper once the fall semester starts. Still, when I make the promise out loud, I immediately know it's a promise I'm going to keep, no matter what. And as I am writing this book a year later, I will smile and look down at my right wrist because I'm still wearing the bracelet. Ricky is right here with me. The COVID pandemic in 2020 will make interstate travel impossible, but I know I will keep my promise and return the bracelet to Masa the first chance I get. True story.

It's getting late, so we say goodbye to all the great people we've met tonight and head back down the mountain towards Casper. Tomorrow morning I will get a tour the Central Wyoming Counseling Center but I'll be doing it solo, since T.C. is catching the red-eye back to Toronto tonight at some ungodly hour. I have to say, it's been great having him here, even for a couple days. We have a last drink at the hotel bar, laughing at some more old stories of our madcap youth before we finally have to say goodbye.

"This is what it's all about," he says, tapping the silver bracelet on my wrist. His voice totally throws me off because for the first time, he sounds serious. "I didn't get that, at first. I just thought you were doing this whole walk thing for the challenge, Tellis, or maybe a midlife crisis. But this," he says, tapping my wrist again. "This is important."

I nod. We finish our beers and meander back towards the elevator, full of great food and even better stories. T.C.'s room is on the third floor, and I'm on the seventh. When he gets out of the elevator, he turns and smiles as the doors close behind him.

"Don't forget," he says, pointing at me one last time. "You're the guy."

Day 69

VALENTINE, NEBRASKA

"**I**T'S ALL downhill from here!" Back in Wyoming, this was just wishful thinking: I'd say that to myself whenever I reached the top of the next ridge or mountain, even though the next climb loomed in the distance ahead. (In Wyoming, it seems like there's always a climb ahead, no matter what direction you choose to go.) But now that I've crossed into the rolling prairie of western Nebraska, I'm saying it because it's true: I've dropped about 4,000 feet in elevation since leaving Casper, and trust me, my lungs are thanking me every single day. Suddenly I feel like I have the lungs of Superman in my chest. And it's perfect timing for my second wind to show up, because when I reach Valentine, Nebraska today, I will officially pass the halfway point of the whole VetZero Walk Across America! It's hard to believe I've come 1,400 miles so far, and just as hard to believe I've still got 1,400 more to go. Maybe the good Lord has finally noticed I paid my dues back in the mountains of Wyoming because walking in Nebraska is turning out to be, well, pretty darn *easy* in comparison. Adding to my delight, the Cornhusker state has handed me a well-maintained walking path called *The Cowboy Trail,* and it's an absolute walker's dream, with a bed of soft red clay, clear markings, and an

arrow-straight trajectory clear across the state for over 195 unin-
terrupted miles. It starts in a little town called Valentine where I
am today, and it runs all the way east to Norfolk, close to the Iowa
border. Right now, things almost feel like they're on cruise control;
the miles pass are passing quickly, save for a random lightning
storm blowing through now and then. I know what you're saying:
knock on wood, big guy. But I'm starting to get comfortable out
here, for the first time. I am starting to realize the hard part of
walking across America isn't the physical part at all. No, the hard
part is the *mental* part, the alone part, the getting-up-and-doing-
it-day-after-day part, knowing you could go home anytime. When
I started this walk, I was so scared of the physical pain of walking
22 miles a day: the blisters, the missing toenails, the knee pain,
the ankle pain, the foot pain. Now I'm halfway through this adventure, and I can say those things don't scare me anymore. In fact, I
rarely even think about them anymore; walking 22 miles in a day
doesn't faze me now.

Turns out, the physical part is actually the easy part. And I can't
believe I'm saying this now, after crawling on my belly to the bathroom after that first day, but the physical part has actually become
the *fun* part. Each day, I wake up and after shaking off a little rust
and stiffness, I honestly look forward to the walk ahead, and what
surprises the day may hold. My legs feel like iron, and my once-
flabby calves now might belong to a bodybuilder.

I've discovered that if you're out here long enough, the mental
part becomes the hard part. For me, the physical pain of walking
has faded a little each day until I hardly notice it – well, most days,
anyway. But when I started, I had a really hard time adjusting to a
new life on the road. Turns out, I had my priorities all wrong. Out
here, there's no deadlines, there's no spreadsheets, there's no conference calls, there's no online networking. There's just me and the
road. Today my life is simple: all I have to do is wake up and walk.
That's my entire 'to-do" list. Tomorrow? Yup, all I have to do is

wake up and walk. And the next day. And the day after that. I had no idea how complicated my old life was, always being connected, always on the treadmill, always on the clock. Out here, there is no clock. There is the sun coming up, and going down. That transition was frightening at first, and it took me a while to adjust and break free from those old constraints that had constantly tied me down. Now? Life is good, actually. I'm actually having fun out here on the low road. Who would have guessed that? Not me, that's for sure. All I had to embrace this new life, and this new *Me*, to become a whole new person. Well, a *better* person, anyway.

Valentine is a sprawling town at the crossroads of US-20 and US-83 in northwest Nebraska that services surrounding farms and ranches with machinery, animal feed and supplies. There's got to be some kind of irony in reaching the heart of my walk in a town named Valentine, but I'm too tired right now to make the connection. As I get closer to town along US-20, I notice the big combines rumbling past me on the highway almost as often as cars or trucks. I've got a mail drop waiting for me at the post office, and I manage to get there an hour before the counter closes. It's been a hot day and I've done twenty miles in the broiling sun, so I must be sight when I lean on the counter, take a deep breath and pull out my ID. They must have been waiting for me; the Postmaster comes out from her office to size me up. "I saw you walking in this morning, out on the highway by Crookston," she says, leaning over the counter to look at my feet. "Looked like you were limping out there."

"Yeah," I say with a nod. "Some days more than others." I tell her the truth: I don't even notice the limp anymore, unless someone else brings it up. These days, standing still for only a few minutes is much more painful than walking, because my feet and ankles and knees don't have time to swell up when they're constantly moving.

Once I stop, though – like right now, standing at the counter in the post office – everything stiffens up within a matter of minutes. All the Advil in the world is not going to fix that.

"We better keep you moving, then," she says helpfully.

The haul from my Valentine mail drop is impressive – not Kemmerer impressive, but there's still too much for one man to carry, and definitely too many Nutter Butters for one man to eat. So I enlist the help of the Postmaster and together, we make a display box out by the front door, where people can take what they like. "I'll keep an eye on it," she says proudly when we're done. "Shouldn't take long to empty. Kids will love it."

But the best surprise I receive today isn't cookies or cake, or any food at all. No, it's the literally hundreds of handwritten cards and letters from young Scouts back home, all with awesome messages like *Go Tommy!* and *Stop Reading My Card, and Walk!* They all make me a little misty when I read them, but I think my favorite is a hand-drawn picture in black crayon that depicts an action scene where stick-figure *"Vetarins"* are taking down a *"Bad Guy"* and saving the world. Yes, A for Effort. As it turns out, Troop 10429 back home in Pleasant Valley, New York put together a summer scouting Jamboree with scouts from all over, and with some help from my social intern supreme Nora, they got all the kids to write something to the big guy in a funny hat walking across America right now. I am beyond floored; I will stand in the post office foyer long after they close today, reading every last one. And in the morning, I will be here when the counter opens again at 7am, so I can send these cards to myself at Marist.

I will never forget receiving hundreds of Valentines in Valentine, Nebraska!

Much later, when I get home to Poughkeepsie, I will hang all of them outside the door of my Marist office for all to see, so that every day at work, I will see our *Vetarins* saving the world, once again. I don't think my neighbors on the third floor of Fontaine

Hall appreciate them as much as I do, but hey, they didn't walk across the country, either. Tomorrow, I will wake up tomorrow with an early start and head out on the Cowboy Trail. A lightning storm will send me running for cover, but no matter; thanks to the encouragement from all the young Scouts and their handwritten cards, my feet feel light for once. After all, it's all downhill from here.

SCHALLER, IOWA

TODAY IS July 4th and here in the Heartland, everything is decked out in festive red, white and blue – but right now, the Fiancée and I are sitting silently in her little rental car on the side of the road in Holstein, Iowa, and we do not feel much like celebrating. Yup, she did end up flying out to Sioux City for the last two days, and I have to say, it hasn't been completely horrible: we've eaten some great food, shared a few laughs, and together, we hung out with some truly awesome veterans in a little town called Correctionville (a name which has nothing to do with prisons – my mistake, proud citizens of Correctionville!). But the whole weekend had a kind of dark storm cloud hanging over it, and I'm not just talking about the weather. It began with one of those hard conversations – you know the kind, when you haven't seen them in a long time – and it's about to end with another as we sit here quietly beside each other in the cool dawn. We're parked next to a Little League field and I can see the morning mist coming up off the shiny, wet grass. She's dropping me off here at oh-dark-early so I can continue the walk, before she drives the forty miles back to Sioux City and catches her morning flight home.

The Fiancée is gripping the steering wheel, hard. The engine is running, we've already had our perfunctory reach-over hug, and my door is wide open, so all that's left to do is for me to reach into the backseat, grab my gear, step outside, say goodbye, and walk away. But we've been sitting here probably for ten minutes, not moving much, not saying a word. She's working up the courage to tell me she's not going to be there on the day I get back to Poughkeepsie on August 23rd. She tells me she's decided to drive down to Virginia instead, to help her Ex move their daughter into college to start the school year. She reaches over and puts her hand on mine. "It's a big moment for her," she says. "It's big for me, too. It's only going to happen once. I don't want to miss that."

"Hey, you've always told me you're a mom first," I say, still looking out at the empty ballfield. "I get it." I think she's expecting me to be angry, but honestly, when she tells me she's not going to be there for me at the end, a big part of me just feels relieved.

"So you think I should go to Virginia?" She looks over at me with her head cocked sideways, like a lawyer slowly circling a witness on the stand, looking for weaknesses. We've been together five years now and engaged for two, so I know that look pretty well. She wants me to say no, of course. She wants me to fight for her. "You think it's a good idea, then?"

"Yes, I do," I say. "Like you said, it only happens once, right?"

Now her head is angled the other way. "And you're not mad?"

"Nope," I say quickly. "Look, you're not going to miss anything when I get back. Even if I make it all the way home, it'll probably end up just being me and Mickey walking through Poughkeepsie alone, then cracking a few beers."

She cracks a smile. "Well, he'd better start training. No way he'll keep up with you now."

I give her another hug and tell her she'd better start back or else she'll miss her flight. I've only got about 18 miles to cover today, so not too bad. It's early, so I can take it easy. Today the end of the road is Schaller, Iowa where I'm supposed to meet the Dad of an old grad school buddy of mine, who's agreed to put me up tonight in the basement of his daughter's house. Yeah, long story. But it beats sleeping in an old cemetery (which incidentally, I will do in a few more days.)

"I'll call you when I get home," she says as I finally get out of the car.

"Sure," I say. "Be safe."

"You, too." She blows a kiss and then turns the compact car around, heading back to the main highway, making a right onto US-20 west towards Sioux City. I watch her go. The car disappears over the hill but I'm still watching. Part of me expects to see the car coming back over the hill, like in a cheesy movie. But it doesn't. I'm not sure what I'm feeling inside, right now. I definitely feel bad, because this is probably all my fault: after all, I'm the guy who suddenly put everything on hold while I walk across the country. I'm the guy who suddenly told my fiancée I wanted to chase windmills. In Cervantes' novel *Don Quixote*, everyone thinks the Don is completely off his rocker as he jousts windmills and follows his imaginary quest – all except for one person, his neighbor Sancho Panza. Sancho agrees to become his squire, even though he probably sees the whole folly just like everyone else. He becomes the one person to champion the Don for his incredible imagination, sense of duty, and immense courage, when everyone else just laughs at the old man's foolish ideas. Without Sancho behind him, Don Quixote never makes it very far in his quest, and his story never gets told.

Looking back, I expected the Fiancée to *want* to be my Sancho Panza. I took for granted that she'd want to share my foolish ideas, when she realized how passionate I had become about making a difference in the lives of our veterans. I just assumed she would fall in love with this new version of me, Tommy 2.0. Instead, when she showed up this weekend in Sioux City, I think she barely recognizes the guy she used to know.

My guts are definitely churning inside as I stand here alone on the side of the road. Am I happy? Am I sad? Did she just break my heart? Did she just set me free? I can't really say for certain.

The only thing certain is I really can't call her the Fiancée, any more.

I wonder how Homer's *Odyssey* would have turned out differently if Odysseus found out Penelope wouldn't be waiting for him back home. Does the quest instantly lose its meaning? Does he keep fighting on the journey home, knowing his true love had already given up on him? I'm imagining our hero Odysseus holding court in some halfway house or roadside bar, far away from Ithaca, singing sailor songs and telling anyone who will listen about the time he almost made it home. *"Got a wife and kids in Ithaca, Jack! I went out for a ride, and I never went back..."*

Is a story still a story, without the ending? Is the hero still a hero? Probably not. But of course, this isn't any normal story. And we've already established that I'm not the hero; that honor is reserved for all the amazing veterans I'm meeting along the way. Heck, this ain't even a normal memoir; it's supposed to be an *anti*-memoir, and now that I think about it, suddenly having no ending sounds oddly appropriate for the long, strange trip we're on. I guess if you call something a Quest for the Holy Fail, you should get used to some disappointment.

Besides, we've come way too far in this quest turn back now.

Now it's late afternoon on Day 81 and I'm standing outside the Sparky's One Stop in Schaller, Iowa, gulping my third Gatorade and chatting with a family clad in bathing suits who recognize me from the local TV news. They're coming back from a sunny day splashing around at North Twin Lake, a popular recreation spot for folks who live here in the deep corn country of central Iowa. I guess you could say I'm officially Iowa famous right now; back in Sioux City, I managed to get my sunburnt mug on the evening news for all four local TV networks (slow news day, I guess) and now, just about everyone on this side of Iowa recognizes the big guy in a funny hat walking through their neck of the woods.

Some folks just want to say hey, and others want to share the story of a veteran they care about. It can make the walking slow, getting stopped all the time, but I don't care; after all, these priceless veteran stories are the reason I'm out here in the first place. This walk is for them! Sure, I might be out here grinding it out on the pavement alone, but every time I hear a new veteran story, I feel like a crowd is walking right behind me.

After a few selfies, the family climbs back in their family truckster and heads back home to celebrate July 4th with a big picnic. I'm pretty hungry myself after this sweaty, eighteen-mile day, but I'm in no hurry; one thing this walk has taught me is patience. The world looks a lot different when you are forced to see it at three miles per hour. Besides, my mind has been occupied all day with a traffic jam of thoughts about the Fiancée and the demolition derby of a weekend we just had. I've had all day to relive each crash and each smoking wreck in slow motion. Nine hours later, I'm just wondering if there were any survivors.

"Are you Tommy?" a voice calls out, pulling me out of my trance. I look up to see an older guy wearing jeans and a checkered shirt, keeping his distance from me in the gas station parking lot.

"You must be Rich," I say, picking up my backpack off the ground when he nods and points out his SUV. My old friend Tim from our days at the University of Alabama has been following the walk on Facebook, and when he saw I'd be walking past his hometown in Iowa, he cajoled his Dad to put me up for a couple nights as I trek across this flat, cornhusky heart of central Iowa.

"Tim called me and told me about your walk," Rich says, breaking the silence. "I told him I'd be happy to help."

"I sure do appreciate it," I say.

"Then he told me you were from New York," he says with a deadpan stare. "So naturally, I told him I'd have to think about it."

I'm just going to say this now: I'm not usually friends with guys like Rich. And truth be told, I'm guessing Rich rarely befriends guys like me. He's a proud farmer who's lived in rural Iowa all his life; heck, the closest I've ever come to a working farm before this walk is watching *Field of Dreams* on cable. Doesn't this sound like the perfect intro to an 80s sitcom? (Does anyone else remember *Perfect Strangers*?) Tonight on ABC! Watch as two guys from opposite worlds are thrown together by unique circumstances – and hilarity ensues! Don't miss it! Followed by *Full House!*

I can actually hear the theme music playing now. *Get out of the city!*

Okay, Rich and I may look like complete opposites, but you know what, we're both proud Americans, and we both care a whole lot about veterans. That's more than enough common ground. We may see a lot of things differently, but when you share the same passion for veterans, well, none of that other stuff really matters that much. And I've met dozens of other folks on this walk with whom I don't share much in common, but once we start talking about veterans and folks in the military, it's like we're old friends.

"You sure are quiet," Rich says as we pass endless rows of corn. "Tim said you were a big, loud kind of guy. I think the word he used was *boisterous.*"

"Whoa, that's a big word for Tim. Doesn't sound like him," I say. I realize I'm talking smack about this guy's own son, right to his face, but I'm slowly figuring out Rich and I share the same weird sense of humor.

Rich cracks a sly smile. "You know, you just might be right."

We pull off the paved road onto a dirt drive that leads to his farm outside Kingsley. I don't want to admit to him this is only the second time I've set foot on an actual, working farm – but I figure he can tell that, already. There's a lot of commotion when we get out of the car: dogs barking, chickens squawking, pigs oinking, cows (these are cows, right?) mooing, all that.

Rich recognizes the bewildered FNG look on my face. "First time on a farm?"

"Are you kidding?" I say with a nervous laugh. "Okay, maybe."

Rich's wife Emily has cooked up a gorgeous meal, and the three of us sit down to a table covered with steaming plates of delicious food. Rich says grace. I can tell he's had plenty of practice.

"I hope you like everything," Emily says modestly.

I'm looking at the food she's made like a kid who just came down the stairs on Christmas. "Ma'am, you're talking to a guy who eats at gas stations. This is *spectacular*." Satisfied with my answer, Emily passes me a china platter heaping with beef brisket, and I stab three or four pieces for my plate. I'm so grateful for this home-cooked meal, but here's a secret Rich and Emily won't know until they read this book: save for that beef braciole Windhorse made back in Oregon, I haven't eaten beef since 2003, when my doctor told me I had about the worst case of gout he'd ever seen. (It still flares up from time to time.) But telling an Iowa farmer you don't eat beef is like telling a Gloucester fisherman you don't eat lobster, so I keep my mouth shut and dig in to the wonderful, delicious meal Emily has prepared. In my three months so far as a homeless veteran, I've learned to check my ego at the door and accept the kindness of strangers.

"I'll take the extra brisket and fix you some sandwiches for your walk tomorrow," Emily says, and I'm already nodding *yes, yes, yes* even before she finishes her sentence. I'm not exaggerating, reader: when you don't know where you'll be able to find your next meal, a homemade sandwich can be worth its weight in gold.

After dinner, Rich gives me a grand tour around Kingsley, the town where he has spent his whole life. We meet a few folks at the body shop downtown, and right away I can tell Rich is super-proud of his hometown. Everyone knows Rich, that's for sure. It's a picturesque little place, the kind of town you'd expect to see on a Christmas card or a Norman Rockwell painting. Instantly I get the feeling veterans and their families hold a very special place in the hearts of the folks who live here. There's a real sense of community here that honestly, I've never experienced back home.

"Tommy, do you like music?" Rich asks out of the blue as we drive around.

"Uh, sure," I say, expecting him to turn on the radio or put in a CD.

Instead, he just nods his head vigorously. "That's good," he says, before taking a deep breath and diving into an old Tom T. Hall novelty song called "Who's Gonna Feed Them Hogs?" which, as you might have guessed, is about a guy laid up in the hospital who needs someone to stop by his farm and feed the hogs. He's singing at the top of his lungs. I think he's trying to surprise me, or maybe embarrass me, with this sudden outburst of a down-home country song – but little does Rich realize I actually know this very song well! My own Dad has always been a big old-time country music fan, and we would sing along to Tom T. Hall, Charlie Rich, Conway Twitty, Mickey Gilley and Mel Tillis on an antique radio in our basement back in the Bronx while we did wood-working projects together. So when I start singing along with Rich, word for word, he shoots me a look of amazement, like Jesus or Elvis just jumped in the backseat behind us. We end up singing the whole song together as we drive around Kingsley.

"We're going to get along just fine," he says with a wry smile. I think I've finally earned his stamp of approval.

Rich stops the car in front of a memorial, and we get out to take a closer look. Rich tells me the inspiring story behind it: a local kid named Chad was KIA in Iraq in 2008. His family holds a golf tournament in his memory each year, distributing the proceeds to organizations that help veterans and military families. It's a powerful moment for me, standing over the memorial plaque for this local kid who used to play ball in the municipal field right behind me, who would go on to give his life in service of his country. Any way you slice it, that's a hero, to me. Later, after I get home, I'll get a letter from Chad's family thanking me for the VetZero mission. They include a picture of Chad from his time in Iraq, and the picture will hang right over my computer screen in my office as I write this book. I'll never forget this moment, because it will always be a solemn reminder of the enormous hole left by heroes like Chad who leave their families and hometowns to serve their country, but don't come back. We can never repay that debt, but we have an obligation to never forget their sacrifice.

Rich and I get back in the car and he takes the next right, onto a normal-looking residential street. There's a development of houses up ahead. For some reason, he stops the car abruptly. "See that?" he says with a broad smile as he points behind us to the street sign on the corner. "You're on Easy Street." Sure enough, when I turn around in my seat I can see the sign literally says *Easy Street*.

I smile. "My feet feel better already."

"I didn't want you to leave Kingsley without being on Easy Street."

"Hey, you know what? It's all downhill from here."

I know, I know: we sound like an out-of-practice comedy team. But I'm grateful for my time getting to know Rich, his family, and his hometown. Not only did they help me re-focus on the reason I'm out here in the first place, they also gave me a much-needed diversion from the sour knot I've had all day in my stomach, thinking about the Fiancée.

Or is it ex-Fiancée, now? Baby steps, Zurhellen. Baby steps.

It's been a long day. Rich drives me over to his daughter's house so I can meet everyone and commandeer their spacious basement, where it will take me about twelve seconds to fall asleep. "Happy

Independence Day," Rich says before he heads back to the farm for the night.

I nod. "You can say that again."

In the morning, Rich will come by bright and early to pick me up and take me back to the same Sparky's One Stop in Schaller, so I can continue the walk. He will be packing some thick brisket sandwiches from Emily, a few bottles of water, and a few more verses of that Tom T. Hall song. I'll be grateful for all the help. And I'll be ready to sing along.

Day 95

BELOIT, WISCONSIN

TODAY IS Homecoming Day at Beloit College! Okay, okay, not really: it's the middle of July, and the tree-lined paths that crisscross the beautiful campus are completely empty, so that's pretty much a bald-faced lie. But today sure feels like a homecoming of sorts to me, because I'm returning to my alma mater where I spent the best four years of my life, back in the late 80s. There are lots of great memories here for me, but it's safe to say, when I imagined my triumphant return to my old stomping grounds, I never imagined it would be on foot. The Beloit campus looks much the same as when I left it in 1991, with a few updates. My fraternity house is still standing on frat row – minus the burnt couch on the lawn. And the ancient brass bell I had to run to from the fraternity house at dawn – naked – to complete my Sigma Chi initiation, that's still here, too. True story. And on the edge of town is Strong Stadium where I played football for three years, on and off.

Mostly off.

You may ask, how did a city kid from the boogie down Bronx end up spending four years at a tiny college out here, smack dab in the middle of the quiet Wisconsin prairie? Well, that's yet another book. But after fifty years making mistakes, I do believe life is just series of detours, backup plans and wrong turns – hey, just like this little stroll I'm on right now. Imagine how boring our lives would be if they actually followed the prefabricated plans we make, without any surprises. At graduation, I tell my writing students at Marist they don't need a map for what lies ahead, because they *are* the map. They have to let life write on them in broad strokes. That's good medicine for all of us, most of all myself. Which is why I'm still out here following the low road, I think.

Last night they put me up in the guest house on campus. They asked what I wanted to do for breakfast this morning; I got some weird looks when I said I'd love to eat at the student cafeteria, which is still in the basement of Chapin Hall. What can I say, I'm a cheap date. The dining hall looks pretty much the same, although I'm bummed there's no sandwich station, like there was when I attended thirty years ago. I think I lived off of the sandwich station for so long, my body is still made out of bologna and processed cheese. At least, it sure feels like it.

After I scarf down some eggs-to-order (a luxury we definitely didn't have when I was a student here, back in the stone ages) and cereal (in the little boxes! I miss those little boxes) I'm scheduled to meet some current Beloit students back at the Alumni office before we kick off a community walk. The students are gracious and polite, but they're looking at me like I'm a dusty exhibit from a roadside museum. They seem a lot more able and a lot more put together than I remember being when I was their age, roaming these same halls. I want to show them the patch of grass where I woke up face down in the mud after a really big night at Folk n' Blues. I want to show them the dorm room in Chapin Hall where I slept through my History final. I want to take them down to Goody's and order boilermakers and play shuffleboard, but Goody's closed years ago. I think these Beloit students are much more into weird things like, you know, reading books and talking about global issues. Yes, the kids are all right.

The Beloit PR office has lined up more TV interviews for today, and by now I'm an old hand at this. I've got ready answers to their questions, and I know exactly what they mean when they say they'd like to get some B-Roll footage. Tonight I'll be on the local news in Janesville, Rockford and Madison, and one of those interviews will get me a call from a Milwaukee morning show, which will really start the ball rolling when it comes to my fifteen minutes of fame this summer.

Being here at my alma mater is bittersweet for me, I think. On the one hand, it reminds me that I've come so far already – almost two thousand miles – and that home isn't so far away. But it also reminds me that I've still got a long way to go: 800 miles to be exact, with a top speed of three miles per hour. When I was a student here, my good buddy and football teammate Chris and I would drive back and forth from New York to Beloit in one fell swoop, usually in the dead of night. The drive would take about seventeen hours total, but we were probably averaging about a hundred miles per hour on the Interstate in my 1978 Caprice Classic coupe.

The next morning, the school has organized a bit of a sendoff rally for me on campus, before I begin the next leg from Beloit to Janesville. It's early, but about thirty or so local folks have shown up to walk the first couple of miles with me along the Rock River and Route 51. There's a sort of receiving line in front of the Alumni house and I feel a bit like royalty standing here as I shake everyone's hand and try to say something pithy. (I'm sure I don't smell much like royalty.) It's fun meeting everyone, but one person stands out from the crowd, a guy wearing a veteran ballcap. I see him out on the sidewalk, waiting patiently with what looks like a walking stick, almost as tall as he is. When I've met everyone the guy comes up, introduces himself as Richard, and presents the stick to me.

"I made this for you," he says proudly, putting it in my hands.

I have to say, reader, this is like the Cadillac of walking sticks, adorned with a rope handle, a rubber cap, and decorated with all the different service branches in red, white and blue paint.

"I've been following your walk for a while," Richard says. "I've been trying to figure out how I can help. I'm not much of a walker, but I am a woodworker. So I figured you could use this." It's a huge stick, but surprisingly very light in my hand. "I knew you were tall, but I couldn't tell *how* tall. So I just made an educated guess."

"Perfect fit," I say. I thank my new friend profusely, and I leave Windhorse's stick in the Alumni house, where (as far as I know) it will stand there in a corner until I can come back and retrieve it. The time has come to shove off, and with Richard's awesome walking staff and a crowd of chatty, excited people walking behind me, I kind of feel like the guy in *The Music Man*, leading folks on a parade march through town. We all walk the first couple of miles together until we reach the Henry Avenue Bridge; after a few group pictures, everyone turns around and heads back to campus, leaving me to finish the day alone.

Thanks for your amazing gift, Richard.

Fun side-note: in my sophomore year at Beloit, I remember we were all very excited because a new chain restaurant called Taco Bell had opened in our little town, right across from the Henry Avenue Bridge. This was edgy cuisine for us, back in 1988. I'm happy to say it's still there. I would stop in now to relive some of those post-game memories, but it's too early, and I'm losing daylight on today's walk.

Tonight I'll drop into the VFW in Janesville for a quick beer on my way into town. It's been a hot day but I've met some great veterans along the way, including a young female veteran who told me about her time in the Army while we sat in the air-conditioning of a gas station, but who wouldn't give me her name. The Janesville

VFW has a Vietnam-era fighter plane and tank standing in the front lawn, so it's no surprise when no one here is particularly impressed with a big guy in a funny hat, walking across America. At least the beer is cold. The sun is going down so I'll take a selfie with the big plane and finish up the last couple of miles for the day, looking for a cheap motel out by the Interstate.

I've got my feet dunked into two tubs of ice (thank you, guy at the Comfort Inn) when Christa pops up on my phone. "Hey CEO," I say. I've gotten used to calling her that, quite frankly because she's the only CEO I know. "How are things back in Poughkeepsie?"

"Everything's good, Commander. I'm calling because I have an idea."

"Let me guess. You want me to walk backwards the rest of the way."

"No, silly. Listen, I want to turn your last mail drop into something special."

And this, dear reader, is how one of my all-time favorite ideas will be hatched: over the phone, in my underwear, chest covered in crumbs from Kentucky Fried Chicken, feet covered in ice. The plan is simple: instead of asking our Facebook followers to send me letters and snacks at our next mail drop in Michigan, we'll ask everyone to send restaurant gift cards to give out to veterans in Flint, Michigan.

You'd have to be living under a rock to not know the people of Flint have been suffering a long time, even before the water crisis began in 2014. But just in case, here's the skinny version: Flint, the birthplace of General Motors, once had a population of 200,000 but due to constant economic setbacks that number has been cut in half. Most of those folks are African-American, and about 45% of residents live below the poverty line. And then it got even worse when the city decided to switch its water supply from Detroit to the Flint River in order to save money. The results were disastrous. Thousands of Flint residents, including many kids, began to get sick from lead and harmful chemicals in their pipes and drinking water. The pipes are slowly being replaced. Lawsuits are still ongoing today. This isn't happening in a city halfway across the globe. This is happening in America. This is happening to our fellow Americans.

I've followed this tragic story for years, and when I first started planning the walk, I knew right away I wanted to include Flint on the itinerary, because I wanted to see their story, first-hand. I wanted to meet these resilient folks myself. As it turns out, Christa is equally passionate about this example of environmental injustice. (She's run an organization for the last twenty years whose sole mission is to empower folks in Poughkeepsie who have been disenfranchised, so I guess the writing was on the wall.) So Christa decided to stop watching from a distance, and actually do something about it. Long story short: her organization Hudson River Housing in Poughkeepsie is part of a nationwide network of community nonprofits called NeighborWorks. And sure enough, Flint is home to a NeighborWorks affiliate. So after a few phone calls, Christa got a hold of her counterpart in Flint, a lawyer named Brian and she pitched an idea to create an event for veterans at the community center in Flint, where I'll give out all the restaurant gift cards to any veterans in need.

"Brilliant plan," I say. "I'm all in."

"I'm all in, too," she says, taking a deep breath. "That's why I'm coming out to Flint. We'll do it together."

MILWAUKEE, WISCONSIN

A LL RIGHT, Mr. DeMille. I'm ready for my close up.

I've done plenty of TV and newspaper interviews so far on this journey from Boise, Idaho all the way to Beloit. Indeed, standing in front of a camera or microphone on the side of the road has almost become second nature. But today will be my first appearance on an actual TV show, in an actual TV studio. *The Morning Blend* in Milwaukee has invited me into the studio for an interview with co-host Molly Fay, to talk about the walk. I'm ushered into the green room by an intern, where the show's producer, a tall woman named Pam, is talking with a couple of young guys who look like identical twins. She can't get a word in edgewise, so she turns to greet me warmly. "You must be Tom. You're on next," she says on the way out. I'm sandwiched between a performance by a local bluegrass band and these two guys, who I am going to name Brad and Chad. Apparently, they are promoters for a summer music festival – I can't really tell for sure, since they're both talking to me at the same time. I ask if they're brothers, but they both laugh and say no.

"We get that," Chad says. "A lot," Brad says.

These guys sure look like brothers; they even have the same

haircut and matching outfits. And apparently, they finish each other's sentences. It's only eight in the morning but they both seem hopped up on plenty of Red Bull and espresso.

"What are you here for, bro?"

"I'm walking across America," I say. They both laugh.

"He's a comedian," Brad says. "Great, we're following a comedian." Now he's got a pained look on his face. "They say, never follow a comedian on these shows, bro."

"Wait, I don't think he's a comedian," Chad says, taking a closer look at my ornate walking stick. "I think he's being serious."

"I'm pretty serious," I say.

Brad throws his hands up. "Are you kidding me, bro? I *love* this guy!"

I spend the next few minutes trying to convince these two clowns I'm not a comedian. I'm not doing a very good job, because whenever they ask me a question about the walk, they're waiting for a punchline. They're convinced my walking stick is some kind prop for my act, and my funny hat is – well, a funny hat.

I try to change the subject. "So, you guys are promoting a music festival?"

They both nod. "Are you local, bro? We're looking for someone to intro the acts."

I close my eyes, rubbing the bridge of my nose. "Like, a comedian?"

"Bingo."

"Look, I'm really walking across the country," I sigh. "For veterans."

"God Bless America. See? I *love* this fucking guy," Brad says. "Like Bob Hope. You're perfect. You got a business card, bro?"

Pam the producer ducks her head in and I'm already standing up, hoping she's here to rescue me. But no. "Five more minutes, Tom. Sorry, they're just starting the song now, then a break, then you. I'll come back for you." She closes the door. I let out a deep breath, still trapped in the fifth ring of Hell, being interrogated by two characters from *Entourage*.

Brad has his arms folded over his chest. "So where do you sleep, out there?"

I shrug my shoulders. "Anywhere I can."

"Ha," Chad says, leaning forward in his chair like a TV detective who's finally found a flaw in the perp's alibi. "Where did you sleep last night?"

Lord in Heaven, I can't take these fucking guys anymore. Not today. So, forgive me for what I am about to do. "Last night?" I say. Now I'm leaning forward, too, and I look him straight in the eye with a deadpan stare that'd make Christopher Walken jealous. "Last night I slept at your mom's house."

There's a long pause before Brad lets out a big laugh. "Damn, he got you, bro. He got you good. See? I *told* you he's a comedian." He points at me. "You're good, bro."

Right on cue, Pam swoops in again to escort me to the studio.

Chad stands up, still not satisfied. "Pam, is this guy a comedian, or what?"

"I don't know," she says, without missing a beat. "I haven't seen his act." Out in the hallway, I compliment Pam on her comedic timing.

"Thirty years in show business," she says as we walk. "You need a sense of humor."

The TV interview itself goes by in a blur. I'm positioned on a huge purple couch next to the host, Molly Fay. Somehow, they've found that grisly picture of my bloody feet on Facebook and we get a few laughs out of that as I tell a couple of sordid stories from the road. Molly is a true pro and makes the interview really easy. (I guess if you live in the Milwaukee area, this is all old news, because Molly Fay has been regarded as Milwaukee's very own Kelly Ripa for a long time.) We talk for a few minutes during the break as they're setting up the cameras for our interview. Molly tells me she's lost someone to suicide in her life, so the Walk Across America is important to her. "Are you nervous?"

I nod sheepishly. I'm fidgeting like I've got fleas – which of course, I probably do. "Yeah, can I be honest?"

"Hey, you're the guy walking across the country," she says cheerily as we're just about to roll camera. "You can be anything you want." That immediately put me at ease, and later tonight when I watch a video of the show, I'll see the relief in my own eyes about two minutes into the interview, when I realize I'm going to make it through this whole thing without stuttering, or stumbling. Or vomiting.

After we're done I thank Molly and then make a bee line for the studio exit; after all, I've still got a ten mile walk across town to the ferry terminal, and then another ten miles to finish out the day in Muskegon, Michigan on the other side of the lake. But before I can escape, Brad and Chad are waiting for me by the door. They watched the whole interview and now they won't let me leave the building without a hug. "We love the vets," Brad says. So the three of us hug it out before Pam hustles them over to the purple couch for the next segment.

"We were watching," Chad says. "So proud of you, bro."

"Yeah, sorry we thought you were joking," Brad says. "You've got to admit, you *are* pretty funny, though."

Everyone knows that quote from legendary coach John Wooden: "The true test of a man's character is what he does when no one is looking." And let's face it, for the entire first half of this wild adventure, no one was looking. Sure, I talked with a few folks here and there on the side of the road, but from the very first day in Portland all the way out to Sioux City, Iowa, nobody besides a few friends really cared about a big guy in a funny hat walking across America alone, because nobody really knew about it. And you know what? Flying (or in this case, walking) under the radar like that for those first three months really tested my character more than anything. After all, I could've packed up and gone home anytime and nobody would have cared all that much. What kept me going? Honestly, I think it was waking up every day to face that true test Wooden is talking about. There is something noble in that. I wanted to find out for myself, at fifty years old, what kind of character I really have. I wanted to see if I was actually someone who could walk the walk, instead of always talking the talk. No spotlight, no media frenzy. In essence, the only person watching me in those first few months was *me*, and that made all the difference.

As I walk out of the TV studio into the bright morning sunlight, I try to quickly find my bearings in an unfamiliar city. I'm amazed how quickly things have changed; just a few weeks ago, the most interest I could hope for in my walk was a random car stopping and the driver asking, "What the hell you doing out here?" Today I just did a morning show in Milwaukee and by the time I find a place to sleep tonight, I'll have completed a couple more interviews over the phone. "Thing are heating up!" Julia says to me all the time, as she sends media request after media request. I know I should be grateful for all this new attention, and I am. After all, I'm out here to raise awareness on veteran suicide and veteran homelessness in our country. But part of me yearns for the early days of this journey when no one was looking.

Turns out, I got used to being the invisible man.

With a little help from my phone, I locate a main drag called Cesar Chavez Drive and follow it south through the heart of downtown Milwaukee, all the way to the waterfront. As I walk this beautiful city, I'm constantly surrounded by bustling mobs of people but at the same time, I feel very alone. Lost in a crowd, indeed. In fact, I feel more loneliness at this moment than I did walking the backroads of Idaho or Nebraska without another human in sight.

That conundrum forces me to mull over John Wooden's classic proverb in my mind once again: "The truest test of a man's character is what he does when no one is looking." I've always taken its truth for granted ever since I heard it from my high school football coach, back in the Bronx. But now I'm thinking it might be a bit more complex than that. I'm wondering which is a truer test of character: doing something when no one is looking, or doing it when *everyone* is looking?

Well, sports fans, we're about to find out! Because one of the people who happens to sees my *Morning Blend* segment is a producer for *NBC Nightly News with Lester Holt*, back in the Big Apple. And in a few more days, I'm going to get a call from New York asking if I would be interested in walking the walk for their cameras – this time, while several million people are looking.

So much for being invisible.

Day 103

GRAND RAPIDS, MICHIGAN

I'M WALKING through the hipster district of downtown Grand Rapids when I come across Arizona Mike. I know it's the hipster district because I see a lot of young, college-aged people wearing silly hats, and also because I just shelled out six bucks for a black iced coffee. Arizona Mike is a homeless veteran who is selling homemade walking sticks on the street corner outside the coffee shop. He's got a few sticks spread out on a blanket next to a sign that reads *US Navy Veteran – Walking Sticks and Canes.*

"That's a real beauty," he says, pointing at the red, white and blue staff I'm carrying around, which Richard made for me back in Beloit. "Can I see it?" I hand it over and he lowers his sunglasses to take a closer look. "Great craftsmanship," he says in awe. "I couldn't make something like that." (If you're still reading, Richard, there you have it: the official Arizona Mike stamp of approval on your woodwork.)

We strike up a conversation, and it turns out we have a lot in common. We're both old sailors, for starters. We're both about the same age. And we're both far from home. Arizona Mike tells me he's originally from Texas (no, I didn't ask) but he came up to Michigan years ago for work; things fell apart, but he never left.

It's a familiar story I've heard more than once on this journey across America. We talk a little more, and for the first time on this walk, I realize one more similarity we share.

We're both homeless veterans, too.

That might seem pretty obvious. After all, haven't I been out here on my own for the last 100 days, grinding it out on the low road, gaining honest experience on what it's really like to be a homeless veteran in America today? Yes. But this is the first time I actually *feel* like a homeless veteran, instead of merely pretending to live like one. There's a huge difference between the two; it's the same wide distance between sympathy and empathy. As I talk with Arizona Mike on this street corner, we're speaking as equals. If I had met him at the beginning of the walk, I know I wouldn't have seen him as an equal. No, I would have automatically looked down at him, as we do with all our homeless folks in America. I would have used the same tired stereotypes we all use when we see someone living on the street. Back then, I would have offered him sympathy, which is something nobody really wants. Sympathy is saying to a person, "I feel sorry for you." But empathy is something completely different. Empathy is saying to that same person, "I understand the pain you are feeling, because I have felt it, too." Empathy is always earned, while sympathy is not. For the longest time on this journey, I had felt like I hadn't earned anything, even after all the trials and tribulations of walking this walk alone. Even when I was sleeping outside on a freezing night, somehow I felt like I was only pretending to know the unique pain of being a homeless veteran.

After almost 2,000 miles, I finally feel like I have begun to earn that empathy, thanks to my conversation with Arizona Mike. I just met the guy, and yet, we're talking like old friends. We're talking on the same level because we have common experiences. We talk for another half-hour, telling each other sea stories, horror stories, love stories and any other kind of story we feel like sharing.

They're all the same story, really: these are *our* stories, and deep inside we know they're worth their weight in gold, because we earned them. As we talk and laugh, I notice other folks streaming by on the busy sidewalk, some tossing a dollar bill or change into Mike's bowl as they pass us by. When the look down, they probably see two homeless vets sitting on the curb, chatting up a storm. That is, if they see us at all.

When I reach out to shake his hand, Arizona Mike looks puzzled at first, even behind his mirror sunglasses. I can tell it's been a while since someone has asked to shake his hand, man to man, vet to vet. After a moment he raises his hand and smiles a crooked smile. "Be safe," he says as we shake hands. "It's a wild world out there."

It is a wild world, indeed. Thanks for the scuttlebutt, shipmate.

I'm still wandering around the hipster district of town when I get a call from Julia back at Marist. She's the Director of Media Relations for the college, and she's been doing a fantastic job for me this whole summer, drumming up local media interest in the walk. If I didn't have Julia and Nora working the phones and social media, it's clear I wouldn't have gotten far, and I probably wouldn't be writing this book right now.

Julia sounds very excited. "Are you sitting down?"

I fall into a bench outside some government building. "I am now. What's up?"

"I got a call from a producer at *NBC Nightly News*," she tells me. "She saw you on that Milwaukee morning show. She wants to do a story on you and the walk."

I sit up straight. "As in, the *NBC Nightly News*," I say. "With Lester Holt."

"That's the one," Julia says, almost singing it; she already knows Lester Holt is a big hero of mine. "The producer's name is Marla. She wants you to give her call. Today, if possible."

I sit up on the bench. "So, wait. This is like, the call."

"Well, it might be more like the call *before* the call. But yes. Are you excited?" The phone slips out of my hand and clatters onto the bench beside me. "Tommy?"

Day 108

FLINT, MICHIGAN

IT'S TURNING into another scorcher of a day as I chip away at the 22 miles from Owosso to Flint along the arrow-straight Corunna Road. Yesterday I walked into the little Owosso post office right before it closed, with my fingers crossed. Nora informs me people are really excited on Facebook about our idea to bring 100 restaurant gift cards to the veterans in Flint – but who knows how much that social media excitement will translate into folks actually taking the time to buy a gift card and put it in the mail. I have to admit, I'm pretty nervous when I approach the counter. I can't show up in Flint tomorrow without the 100 cards we promised. I don't want to disappoint any of the veterans we'll meet, and even worse, I don't want to disappoint Christa. The line at the Owosso post office is moving very slowly. There's only one person working the counter this late in the day, an older woman with thick glasses and a permanent scowl. Even from back here, I can tell she's a no-nonsense kind of gal.

A tall, lanky guy in his 20s with long, blonde Viking hair and a backwards USPS ballcap comes out from the back. When he spots me at the counter with my big stick and funny hat, his eyes get real wide, like he's spotted a UFO. "Hey, Lou, that's the guy."

The woman at the counter turns around to face him with an annoyed look, and then turns back to me. "Are you the guy?"

"I think I'm the guy," I say. "I'm the guy picking up General Delivery mail?"

"Yep, he's the guy, all right," the Viking kid says, already darting into the back room. "I knew it, Lou."

"You must be Lou," I say.

She nods slowly. "That's Calvin," she says, rolling her eyes. "He's been waiting to meet you all week." Calvin comes back out juggling stacks of cards, letters and small packages. There's a lot of them; maybe there's a hundred, maybe not. I can't tell. Calvin dumps them on the counter, and then finds me a couple of shopping bags to help haul them away.

I tell Lou and Calvin the story about the gift cards for veterans in Flint, and even Lou seems impressed. Well, a little. "We're closing in a few minutes," she says with a yawn. "But if you want, you can stick around here and open your mail. Calvin will find you a chair. Beats standing out in the waiting area, I guess."

"Great idea, Lou," Calvin says. "I'm sticking around to see if you make 100."

I hunker down at one of the tables and start tearing through all the envelopes. After an hour, I'm done. I could've finished earlier, but lots of folks wrote inspirational messages inside their cards and letters, and I want to take my time reading them all. Calvin keeps popping his head in from the back room every few minutes.

"So, how many did you get?" he says. "Enquiring minds want to *know*, dude."

"Ninety-nine, exactly," I say with a big smile and a sigh of relief. There's cards for every chain restaurant from Burger King to Olive Garden, sent by folks all over the country who are following the VetZero Walk Across America on Facebook. I'm getting a little misty, sitting here thinking about so much kindness being sent by complete strangers all over the country to help veterans in Flint, Michigan. I have to say, it lifts me up. It makes the walking easy.

"That's a lot of people who want to help," Calvin says. "That rocks, dude." Calvin my man, I couldn't agree with you more. You rock, dude.

He insists on taking a picture of me and Lou in front of the post office, for posterity's sake. Somehow, Lou obliges him. Then I stuff up my gift-card treasure hoard into my backpack and say goodbye to my new friends. I stop by the local Walmart to pick up one more restaurant gift card to make it an even hundred before finding a bed for the night. There's a combination motel/carwash (not a typo!) down the main drag from the Walmart, which seems just about perfect for a guy like me: if I don't get a good night's sleep, at least I can get squeaky clean, with a wax job, to boot. I call Christa from the motel/carwash (it's actually kind of delightful) to let her know we indeed have 100 gift cards, on the nose. She tells me she's excited to fly out early in the morning. I'm planning an extra-early start for Flint in the morning myself, for two reasons. One, it's going to be a very hot day. And two? Hey, I simply can't wait to get there.

Flint, Michigan probably isn't first on your list of must-see destinations in America. If you're a tourist driving the kids around on the great American road trip, it's likely to be the last. But if you're walking the low road, trust me, this is the one part of the real America you definitely don't want to miss. Yes, it's got the highest crime rate in the country. Yes, the unemployment rate is doubled here. And yes, you can't even drink the water.

These might be reasons for most folks to avoid a place like Flint, Michigan. But for me, it's the exact opposite: these are the reasons I couldn't wait to come. Let's face it, some people run away from a storm, and other people run into it, hoping to do some good, hoping to help their fellow woman or man. That's not courage, or recklessness, or bravado. That's just empathy. I've learned enough about the power of empathy on this walking adventure to last two lifetimes.

And I've been out here too long to run away from a storm, ever again.

A story of environmental injustice and really bad decisions, the Flint Water Crisis began back in 2014, when the city switched its drinking water supply from Detroit's system to the nearby Flint River, to save money. Inadequate treatment and testing of the water resulted in a series of major water quality and health issues for Flint residents— issues that were chronically ignored, over-looked, and discounted by government officials even as complaints mounted that the foul-smelling, discolored, and off-tasting water piped into Flint homes for 18 months was causing skin rashes, hair loss, and itchy skin. The Michigan Civil Rights Commission, a state-established body, concluded that the poor governmental response to the Flint crisis was a "result of systemic racism."

Later studies would reveal that the contaminated water was also contributing to a doubling—and in some cases, tripling—of the incidence of elevated blood lead levels in the city's children, imperiling the health of its youngest generation. It was ultimately the determined, relentless efforts of the Flint community—with the support of doctors, scientists, journalists, and citizen activ-ists—that shined a light on the city's severe mismanagement of its drinking water and forced a reckoning over how such a scandal could have been allowed to happen.

Long before the recent crisis garnered national headlines, the city of Flint was eminently familiar with water woes. For more than a century, the Flint River, which flows through the heart of town, has served as an unofficial waste disposal site for treated and untreated refuse from the many local industries that have sprouted along its shores, from carriage and car factories to meatpacking plants and lumber and paper mills. The waterway has also received raw sewage from the city's waste treatment plant, agricultural and urban runoff, and toxics from leaching landfills. Not surprisingly, the Flint River is rumored to have caught fire—twice.

As the industries along the river's shores evolved, so too did the city's economy. In the mid-20th century, Flint—the birthplace of General Motors—was the flourishing home to nearly 200,000 people, many employed by the booming automobile industry. But the 1980s put the brakes on that period of prosperity, as rising oil prices and auto imports resulted in shuttered auto plants and laid-off workers, many of whom eventually relocated. You might have seen this play out in Michael Moore's searing documentary *Roger & Me*, which came out in 1989. Since then, the city found itself in a precipitous decline: Flint's population has since plummeted to just 100,000 people, a majority of whom are African-American, and about 45 percent of its residents live below the poverty line. Nearly one in six of the city's homes has been abandoned.

This was the lay of the land in 2011, when Flint, cash-strapped and shouldering a $25 million deficit, fell under state control. Michigan Governor Rick Snyder appointed an emergency manager (basically an unelected official chosen to set local policy) to oversee and cut city costs. This precipitated the tragic decision in 2013 to end the city's five-decade practice of piping treated water for its residents from Detroit in favor of a cheaper alternative: temporarily pumping water from the Flint River until a new water pipeline from Lake Huron was built. Although the river water was highly corrosive, Flint officials failed to treat it, and lead leached out from aging pipes into thousands of homes.

In early 2016, a coalition of citizens and groups—including Flint resident Melissa Mays, the local group Concerned Pastors for Social Action, NRDC, and the ACLU of Michigan—sued the city and state officials in order to secure safe drinking water for Flint residents. Among the demands of the suit: the proper testing and treatment of water for lead and the replacement of all the city's lead pipes. In March 2016, the coalition took additional action to address an urgent need, filing a motion to ensure that all residents— including children, the elderly, and others unable to reach the city's free water distribution centers—would have access to safe drinking water through a bottled water delivery service or a robust filter installation and maintenance program.

Those efforts paid off. In November 2016, a federal judge sided with Flint residents and ordered the implementation of door-to-door delivery of bottled water to every home without a properly installed and maintained faucet filter. A more momentous win came the following March with a major settlement requiring the city to replace the city's thousands of lead pipes with funding from the state, and guaranteeing further funding for comprehensive tap water testing, a faucet filter installation and education program, free bottled water through the following summer, and continued health programs to help residents deal with the residual effects of Flint's tainted water.

But the work of Flint residents and their advocates isn't finished yet. Ensuring that the provisions of the 2017 settlement are met is an ongoing task. Indeed, members of the lawsuit have already returned to court to see that the city properly manages its lead service line replacement program and provides filters for faucets.

I became interested in the story of Flint long before I ever thought about walking across America. In the summer of 2013, my hometown of Poughkeepsie, New York had its own water crisis, after *E. coli* bacteria was found in the city's drinking water. But that only lasted for a few days, and if you simply boiled tap water, you could drink it. It was a nuisance, at worst. In comparison, the Flint Water Crisis has been going on for years, and they can't just boil the lead and deadly chemicals out of their water. I couldn't imagine the conditions the folks in Flint were living in, and I wanted to do something to help. After all, these are fellow Americans, and they deserve our support.

Now, it would be very foolish to think a big guy in a funny hat simply walking through Flint is going to help solve people's problems, like some kind of beefy Pied Piper. We know the world doesn't work like that. But that's not going to stop me from being there to try to lend a hand in any way I can. Sometimes being a witness is the most valuable assistance you can give. Sometimes listening to the stories that need to be told is worth more than any bailout or government program. The people of Flint have been working really hard to make their community a better place long before I set foot there, and they're going to keep working hard, long after I am gone.

I'm walking down Martin Luther King Avenue in downtown Flint, trying desperately to find the Catholic Charities center on Chippewa Street, where this grand shindig is going to be held. I'm a little lost, and I'm going to be late. A few minutes ago, I picked up a local TV crew as I crossed over the Flint River on the Saginaw Street Bridge; the camera guy is making a valiant effort to avoid tripping on the sidewalk as he walks backwards, a few feet ahead of us. The young reporter walking with me asks if we could slow down, but I don't want to be late. Finally I see the Chippewa Street sign up ahead. Left? Right? Who knows. When I make a left, I am immediately surprised by an angry mob of protesters choking the whole street ahead. There's people shouting at the top of their lungs, waving signs, and shoving fists in the air, so I figure they must be protesting something. Even the camera guy stops to take a closer look. But after a few seconds of debating whether or not to go back, I spot Christa in a red dress in the middle of the crowd, cheering as loud as anybody.

"I was worried no one would show," I yell into her ear.

"Are you kidding? Look around! You're a rock star."

The event Christa and Brian have put together turns out to be wonderful. A lot of local veterans show up, and we have inspirational speeches and testimonials from all sorts of folks who are trying their best to raise Flint up, a fiery Phoenix from the ashes. And I get to spend a lot of time talking with veterans from Flint, which I love. After the event is over, guys from the local VFW invite Christa and I back to the Post for a cold drink ... and karaoke.

Now, I must mention that although this is my memoir, I've been sworn to secrecy on what will come to be known as the Karaoke Incident. Here's what I can tell you: there was indeed karaoke. There was indeed some form of singing. I can also tell you that the folks at the VFW in Flint, Michigan take their karaoke *very, very seriously*. And I can tell you that years later, Christa and I will still laugh whenever one of us mentions it.

It's getting late, and Christa has an early flight back home in the morning. I've got three days and sixty miles before I reach Detroit. After that, Buffalo. We find a restaurant open late, where we can debrief and decompress after what has turned out to be a glorious, uplifting day for both of us. I think we're both feeling the adrenaline rush from taking a risk, and having it pay off. We're both feeling proud of being able to create something out of nothing, in order to help people in need. I've been out here on the low road long enough to realize empathy is a powerful drug; for my money, I don't know if life gets any more satisfying than helping others, just for the sake of helping. This might sound odd, but I'm realizing kindness is actually like a drug: once you start helping others, you don't want to stop. I know I don't want to stop, even after this walk ends. And judging from the beaming smile on Christa's face right now as we order our food, she doesn't want to stop, either. It's funny, we both already have jobs that help others: I'm a teacher, she runs a nonprofit. But it feels like we've been hit by the same bolt of lightning. And I have to say, it's a refreshing feeling, having someone in my corner who wants to chase windmills just as much as I do.

I'm still wearing my grungy clothes from the walk; I can actually hear the salt from my old sweat crackle on my shirt whenever I move a shoulder. "This place is kind of fancy," I say, looking around at the mostly empty dining room. "And I smell terrible."

Christa shrugs. "I grew up on a farm," she says. "You smell normal to me."

"This has been an amazing day. Thanks for flying out here, and setting it all up." I take a sip of my beer. "That was my first flash mob, you know."

I can see the gears turning inside her head. "You want another one?"

"Of course," I say. "Who wouldn't."

"Good," she says with a devious smile. She leans forward and folds her hands neatly on the table. "Because I'm coming out to Buffalo, too."

CANANDAIGUA, NEW YORK

WE'RE GETTING close to the end. I'm told by the people who know memoirs that this is the part of the book where I need to "start looking for the exits." I'm not exactly sure what that means; it sounds like we should all panic because there's a terrible fire and if we don't find the exits we will all suffocate and die in a towering inferno of flame and smoke. Okay, not really. Seriously, I think it means we should start to bring back elements from the early chapters of the book, to offer a sense of closure and to make the reader feel like we've come full circle. Perfect timing, because today on Day 120 my old shipmate Paul is flying out from Portland to meet me in the town of Canandaigua, for one last day on the trail. Truth be told, I wouldn't let him forget a promise he made back on Day One: if I ever made it as far as Central New York, he would fly out and walk another day with me. He made the mistake of saying it out loud. Now, I don't think Paul considered I'd ever make it this far – and to be honest, I didn't, either. But a promise is a promise, shipmate. Besides, Paul is using this as an excuse to visit some old friends in the area, including his old college buddy Dave who just happens to own a successful microbrewery in (wait for it) Canandaigua, New York.

Perfect timing, indeed!

Walking in my home state of New York for the last several days has been both a blessing and a curse. The blessing is, I know a lot of these roads already, so there's no getting lost; I know where I'm headed, and I know I'm getting close to home. The curse is, I can only go three miles per hour, so after each familiar landmark or road sign I pass, there's an impatient gremlin on my shoulder grumbling, *Why. Are. We. Going. So. Slow.* One half of me can't wait to get back home. The second half can't imagine ever stopping.

And for every mile I get closer to Poughkeepsie, the second half gets a little louder, and a little bolder. So I find myself conflicted.

Detroit was great because I got to walk a full day with some of my cousins, and Buffalo was another media triumph, thanks to Christa and her team from Hudson River Housing driving all the way up from Poughkeepsie to put together an event at the Matt Urban Center, which is named after Lt. Col. Matt Urban, one of the most decorated soldiers of World War II. We got great press coverage at that event, but getting veterans from the local VFWs and American Legions to show up proved once again to be difficult. (I guess I should be used to that, by now.) The next day on my walk from downtown Buffalo to the town of Alden, I'm intercepted on the road by Marla, the producer from *NBC Nightly News with Lester Holt*. We spend a couple hours getting B-Roll footage on the tree-lined streets of Depew, a picturesque Buffalo suburb. When she's packing up the camera gear into her rental car, she says she'll bring a crew to follow me on the day I get back to Poughkeepsie. "And this isn't official yet," she says, lowering her voice. "But it looks like you're on the anchor track."

"Damn," I say. "Well, we tried." Marla may have forgotten I'm an old sailor, so when she says *anchor track*, I'm automatically thinking it's a bad thing: anchors tend to sink. Anchors tend to get thrown overboard and dragged through the muck. Maybe it's producer lingo for *start looking for the exits*, only instead of escaping a fire you're trying not to drown?

"No, it's a good thing," she says. "It means the anchor covers your story that day."

Suddenly, I'm a little starstruck. "So, Lester Holt is going to cover my story."

"If he's anchor that day, yes. But sometimes there's a replacement."

"What I'm hearing you say is, Lester Holt and I are going to be best friends."

She laughs. "Exactly."

I'm walking south along Rochester Road towards downtown Canandaigua when a minivan pulls up beside me and a guy yells out the window. "You'll never make it to Poughkeepsie like that. Holy shit, is that the fastest you can walk?" It's Paul, of course, leaning halfway out the passenger window like a college kid late to a tailgate. His buddy Dave is behind the wheel. From what Paul told me, Dave built Naked Dove Brewing in an old auto repair a few miles outside town, and it's grown into one of the most respected craft breweries in New York – which is saying a lot in this state, considering how many have popped up over the last twenty years. Dave has been gracious enough to put together a VetZero fund-raiser at the brewery tonight, with the big guy in a funny hat as the main attraction. I can't thank him enough for his kindness.

I'm excited to see Paul again. I've got so much to tell him. Heck, the last time I was this excited to see another dude was when I was seventeen and my Dad picked me up at a payphone in the South Bronx at three a.m. True story.

Still leaning out of the car, Paul seems impressed. "You look different, brother."

"I *feel* different, brother."

He nods. "We're headed to the brewery to set up. Want a lift?"

"No way," I say. Two more miles and I'll have a solid twenty for the whole day. "What do you think, Dave? Three miles until I get to Naked Dove?"

"That's about right. When you get to the bottom of this hill, make a left onto Eastern Boulevard," Dave says. "When you smell beer, you must be there."

"Roger that," I say. "I'll see you guys in another hour."

The gravel parking lot at Naked Dove Brewing is jam-packed with cars when I get there. Later tonight, I'll tell Dave I've actually been here before; I stayed at the tropical-themed motel next door when I caught Judas Priest and Whitesnake at some outdoor music festival nearby, about ten years ago. (The motel's plastic flamingos brought me back.) The fundraiser is wonderful, and even if it wasn't, Dave makes such fantastic beers I had no trouble sampling them all. A lot. I get the opportunity to meet some really great folks who have come out to hear about the walk, including a shy young gentleman about nine years old who has made me a keepsake for the rest of my walk: a smooth, painted stone to keep in my pocket as good luck. Thanks, young sir!

Paul and I drink our share of delicious craft beer tonight, but luckily, Dave is our designated driver. Later tonight, we'll crash at his house and tomorrow morning, after a hearty breakfast, Dave will dutifully drive us right back here to the brewery so Paul and I can begin our walk to Geneva, the next town over. This time, I will do most of the talking. I've got so much to tell him. I can't wait to tell Paul about First Blood Day back in McCammon, Idaho. I will tell him about the mountain lions back in Prineville, and the lightning storm in Valentine. I will tell him about Windhorse and Bob and Arizona Mike and all the other amazing veterans I have met along the way.

"Don't leave out anything," Paul will say as we walk. "I want to hear everything."

I will tell him about the weather in Wyoming. I'll tell him everything about Iowa, and I'll tell him all about Flint. I'll tell Paul what it's like to be best friends with Lester Holt – okay, maybe not that. But I'll tell him every detail I can remember, and when we reach Geneva after a solid eight hours of walking, we'll sit under a tree beside Lake Seneca, resting our tired feet and waiting for Dave to find us in the minivan so he can take Paul back to Canandaigua, since he has an early flight the next morning. "I'm glad I made that promise back in Portland," Paul will say as we gaze out at the waves on the lake. "I'm proud to be a part of it. I wouldn't want to miss this, for the world."

Day 123

ITHACA, NEW YORK

TODAY ON the low road there's some good news, and some bad news. First, the bad news: today my walking stick will be stolen in broad daylight. Yeah. It's the one my Dad made for me, so it's got extra-special value. But the good news is, this petty crime will rank as the worst I will experience on the entire walk. Imagine that: I've already walked over 2,000 miles through packed cities and empty deserts, on lonely trails and busy highways, sleeping on the side of the road in a tent or seedy motels, and the biggest complaint I will be able to muster against my fellow Americans when I get home will be that some jerk swiped my walking stick outside a Dunkin' Donuts in Ithaca, New York.

That's unbelievable, and honestly quite shocking, because we live in such a cynical world. Every day we're reminded about the countless things we should be scared about whenever we step outside our door: muggers, mobs, murder hornets, kids in hoodies trying to steal our identities, sex perverts in back alleys trying to steal our kids. The news always seems to be bad news. We're told the people who don't look or think like we do are our enemies, that nine times out of ten, strangers are only out to get us. We get so jaded and just resolve ourselves to accepting the fact we all hate each other. Sound familiar?

Well, I'm here to tell you, that's not the truth at all. In fact, it's the exact opposite of the real America I've witnessed first-hand this whole summer. When I started this journey, I expected to get regularly chased by angry mobs with torches and pitchforks just because I was a weird-looking homeless guy passing through, a stranger in a strange land. But nothing could be further from the truth. I can't tell you how many times complete strangers came up to me and asked if I needed anything, and that was before they discovered I was a veteran walking across America to bring awareness to important issues. The first hundred times that happened, it surprised me. But now I've realized that the real America isn't that divided, cold, uncaring place we're told it is every time we look online or read a newspaper. No, not at all. The truth is, the real America is full of honesty and empathy, from sea to shining sea. The real America is jam-packed with the kindness of strangers. I should know, since I relied on that kindness pretty much every single day out here. And that kindness never once failed me when I needed it.

Well, except for the asshole outside the Dunkin' Donuts in Ithaca, of course.

It's raining hard when I cross the Sixmile Creek Bridge into Ithaca after a very long day walking south along Route 96 from a little town where I stayed last night called Ovid. It's been a 25-mile day, officially the second-longest day of the whole walk, at least according to mileage, and even though the last few miles today were sloped downhill, I'm ready to get off my aching, wet feet. I'm running a little late today; in about five minutes I'm supposed to meet Christa and the folks who run the local shelter to talk about the walk, but I duck into a Dunkin' Donuts to get out of the rain for a few minutes and use the bathroom. As usual, I leave my big stick leaning against a wall outside – I've found that most people behind the counter get startled when a disheveled, 300-pound wizard comes into their business, waving a huge wooden staff around – but when I come back out after two or three minutes, the walking stick is gone. I look around, but nothing. I would do some more snooping around, but I'm late for the event at the community center, a few blocks away.

Somewhere in Ithaca tonight, there's a teen proudly showing off his new wizard staff to his friends, wondering how much weed he could trade for it.

Christa greets me in the parking lot. She's set up the event tonight with the community shelter here in town, since they belong to the same network as Hudson River Housing called NeighborWorks. She gives me a big hug, trying to hold her umbrella over my head even though I'm already drenched, from hat to socks. Then she narrows her eyes a bit, looking at me like something's different. "Did you get a haircut?"

"Nope," I say. "But someone just stole my stick outside the Dunkin' Donuts."

I tell Christa the short version of The Case of the Purloined Walking Stick, and in typical Christa fashion she immediately squares her shoulders, grits her teeth, and says to me in a voice I know must be the voice she uses to terrify her kids.

"All right," she scowls. "Let's go get your stick back."

She's already steaming across the parking lot, back towards the scene of the crime, when I remind her we're already an hour late to this Neighborworks thing, so we should just go inside and forget about it. "Listen, Ithaca P.D. will put out an APB on a six-foot hunk of wood, follow some leads, check out some John Does, maybe even pull in a few favors from the boys uptown," I say in my best old-timey, detective movie accent. "And in a few hours, they'll have this case all wrapped up. You'll see, those perps will be up river making license plates before you can say *jiminy crickets*."

Christa smiles. "You're a funny guy."

"Only to my friends," I say. "To everyone else, I'm fucking impossible."

Now she's laughing out loud. She finally relents, so we turn around in the rain and aim her umbrella towards the door of the community center. Together, we plunge inside, where there's a crowd of about thirty folks waiting patiently to talk with the big guy in the funny hat. My favorite part of the night – well, besides making Christa laugh out loud – is clowning around with the half-dozen little kids that want to see the walker man. A couple of the kids keep saluting me, like every few seconds, and I can't resist saluting them back every time, even when I'm talking to the adults in the room. One of those adults is actually my old grad school buddy Sue, and it'll be great catching up with her afterwards at dinner. She's taught at Ithaca College about as long as I've been at Marist, maybe longer. The people who run the shelter are horrified when they learn about my stolen stick, but I tell them not to worry – hey, if this is the worst thing to happen to me while walking across the country, then I must be doing something right. Besides, when I call my Dad later tonight and let him know the stick he crafted is gone, here's what the old man will say, word for word:

"We'll just have to make you another one, then." Thanks, Dad.

I won't say this out loud, to Christa or my Dad or anyone else, but it's going to be really weird walking out of here without a stick after walking with one for so long – ever since Windhorse gave me his stick way back in Oregon, actually. I've leaned on my stick in a lot of ways since then. Now that I'm without it, I almost feel like I'm missing a limb. Luckily, I have the beautiful red, white and blue walking stick that Richard made for me back in Beloit, waiting for me in Poughkeepsie. All I have to do is find a way to get it up here to Ithaca, New York so I can finish these last 200 miles with all my limbs intact.

Day 129

ELLENVILLE, NEW YORK

O NLY TWO days to go, and today Mickey and Bert from the VFW have come out to walk a stretch with me. Originally, they wanted to walk the whole day, just over 22 miles, but gradually I talked them down to six. Don't get me wrong, I'm happy they want to walk with me, and I appreciate the enthusiasm. But I also know how out of shape they are. I don't want any casualties on my watch, not this close to home. "There's a lot of hills," I say before we start. "So it'll feel a lot longer, trust me." We agree to start at the Dunkin' Donuts parking lot in Liberty where I stopped walking last night, along Route 52. (Of course, I've had bad luck recently outside a Dunkin', with my walking stick being stolen in Ithaca, but I don't tell them that.) When Mickey gets out of the car he immediately starts doing some weird stretches that look like they're from a VHS workout tape made in 1983. He's also wearing camo gear head-to-toe from his Army days, including his bush hat from his time in Saudi Arabia. I can smell the Ben Gay from here. His hiking socks are pulled all the way up to his knees.

Bert whistles at him. "How many pairs of socks you got on?"

"Three," Mickey says, doing side bends. "Unlike you, I came prepared."

"Whatever," Bert says, locking his car and starting towards the highway. "Shall we?"

"Hold on," Mickey says, pointing at the Dunkin'. "We're going to eat first, right?"

It's busy inside but we manage to order and grab a free table. I bring my stick inside with me this time. Bert and I sip our iced coffees slowly while Mickey demolishes a breakfast sandwich and then starts an attack on a half-box of donuts, eating way too fast.

Bert shakes his head. "You're going to get sick."

"I've got to carbo-load," Mickey says, downing his third crème donut, alternating bites with big slurps of coffee, like a professional eater furiously trying to beat the clock. "Tell him, Tom. You know, right? You've got to fuel up, or else you'll run out of gas."

"You're going to run out of something," I say.

"Exactly," Mickey says, his mouth full of brown coffee-and-donut mush.

Okay ladies and gents, here's our marching orders for today: Mickey and Bert will walk the first six miles with me to a remote parking lot where they've stashed Mickey's pickup truck. From there, they'll come back to get Bert's car, and I'll finish the day solo, ending up in Ellenville for a total of 22 miles, on the nose.

The day doesn't start so great; a quarter-mile into the walk, Mickey remembers he left the keys to his truck in Bert's car, back at the Dunkin' parking lot. And then there's the weather: there's dark clouds threatening overhead and the forecast is talking about a chance of showers all day. Bert and I wait on the shoulder for Mickey to fetch his keys, and then the three of us start off again alongside Route 52.

"I don't like the look of those clouds," Bert says.

"Well, at least it's not raining," Mickey says, bringing up the rear. Almost on cue, it starts to sprinkle. Bert looks back and gives him the old stink eye.

Mickey shrugs. "At least it's not raining hard, though, right?"

Sure enough, a few minutes later we find ourselves in the middle of a full-force gale – and apparently, also in the middle of a vaudeville comedy routine, starring Mickey. It only takes a few minutes and we're completely drenched from head to toe; we've still got a few miles left before we hit the cutoff point where we left Mickey's truck. To add insult to injury, the big rigs are dousing us with big waves of water as they pass by. It's turning out to be a miserable day, and I feel bad for these guys who came out to support me.

"Well, at least it's not thundering and lightning," Mickey yells over the rain, and immediately Bert and I both shout, *"Stop talking!"* as we look up at the sky, waiting for a jagged flash of light or a booming thunderclap. Luckily, we seem safe for now.

When we finally reach the cutoff point, it's stopped raining but Mickey is limping and laboring a few clicks behind and Bert looks spent, too, so I'm glad these guys are only doing six miles. Mickey finally catches up and they will drive back to Bert's car in the Dunkin' Donuts parking lot in Liberty, and I will continue on to the next town, Ellenville. It's sixteen more miles but it's mostly flat and downhill with a big shoulder – definitely a walk on Easy Street, compared to some days where I feared I couldn't make it, or worse, feared for my life from dodging oncoming traffic, dogs, and weather.

I look at Mickey. He doesn't look so good. "Are you okay?" I say, wondering if those crème donuts are about to make a return appearance.

"I was just about to get my second wind," Mickey says, leaning over on his knees.

"You want to keep going?" Bert laughs. "I'll follow you guys in the truck."

"That's okay," Mickey says, still breathing hard. "Got to save my strength for tomorrow." Part of my pitch to Mickey and Bert on why they should only do six miles with me today was, they can do another six miles tomorrow, if they feel up to it. I have a feeling they'll both wake up tomorrow morning and beg off from being too sore, but stranger things have happened.

The sun has come out and I'm cruising along, getting close to Ellenville when suddenly, a thought runs through my mind and literally stops me in my tracks; I've just realized that today will be my last 22-mile day for the summer. This is it. Tomorrow will only be sixteen miles, even though it will be hilly, and the next day – the very last day of the VetZero Walk Across America –is a short twelve miles from New Paltz to Poughkeepsie. A walk in the park. A quick stretch of the legs. Easy street.

Then it hits me, all at once: what will you do, the day after that?

I feel so emotional I have to sit down; I throw off my pack and lean on the aluminum railing that guards the highway. Suddenly I don't feel so good. Suddenly my feet feel like they're made out of lead. I can't believe I'm only two days away from the end of this journey. I should be all smiles, ecstatic even, being so close to the end. But I'm not. I'm going to miss it, all of it, the good parts and the bad parts alike. I've been out here on the low road so long that I've almost forgotten that I have a completely different life waiting for me back home, a life with deadlines and meetings and spreadsheets and reports and grading and responsibilities. I actually have to teach class only a few days from now, and I don't even remember my Marist password to open my email. I don't even know what classes I'm teaching. In my mind that world has seemed so distant, but now it's only a few days away. That terrifies me. All those old worries from my previous life I escaped five months ago are coming crashing back with a vengeance, all at once – and Lord, I'm not ready.

I'm not ready to go back.

NEW PALTZ, NEW YORK

T HE NEXT day starts early in the Walmart parking lot in Ellenville. Julia texts me today is the *penultimate* day of the walk, which I have to look up; turns out, it's a fancy way of saying, next to last. I feel better after a good night's sleep in an actual bed. To my surprise, both Mickey and Bert have come back for a second round of punishment, and this time they've even brought along reinforcements: four more adventurous souls from the VFW, eager to tackle a day on the low road. Well, five miles worth, anyway. When I show up at the Walmart, they're already there, doing deep knee bends and drinking green protein smoothies.

"Don't worry," Mickey whispers to me. "I told them about the carbo-loading."

Here's the penultimate plan for today: we've got a rag-tag crew of about eight walking the first five miles, single-file along the shoulder of the highway. When we reach the Valero gas station, everyone will take a break and I'll continue on for another nine miles over the steep Shawangunk mountain. Then we'll all meet up again later this afternoon on the other side, at a German brauhaus which promises authentic German beer and brats. Mickey suggested the brauhaus, naturally.

I'm bringing up the rear of our detail, and we're only a mile down when I see streaks of green protein drink on the asphalt. Looks like a breakfast burrito mixed in there, as well. Two miles into our walk, a reporter from a local newspaper catches up and asks me a few questions as we walk together. She had to make it past my crack security detail – also known as Mickey and Bert – so I figure she's earned this interview, and then some. After a few boilerplate questions, she starts asking the good stuff.

"So, what do you do when you have to go to the bathroom?"

I smile, because that's a whole other book, by itself. "You just go."

"You just go?"

I nod. "You just go."

"You never got arrested or anything?"

"Not yet." I guess I've never thought about it that much, until now. Most of the time I've been so isolated and alone I've never worried about someone seeing me do my business, much less getting arresting me for it. But no, for the record, I've left countless parts of me all across America, all without any hassle.

"Okay, last question," she says, holding up her digital recorder while we walk. I can tell she's nervous about the oncoming traffic. "How do you feel about this all ending, tomorrow?"

"Honestly?" I say. "Terrified."

It's a sunny, warm day and the route is pretty flat, so our little band covers the five miles to the gas station without any problems. Everyone is feeling pretty good, even though they can't remember the last time they walked five miles. "I'm going to be sore tomorrow," someone says. We all nod our heads in agreement.

Well, except for Mickey. He's standing with his arms folded. "This was nothing. You should have been out here yesterday, with me and Tom and Bert. We did six miles, and the hills were like this," he says, holding his arm straight up. "Rain, sleet, big trucks going by like you wouldn't believe. Now that was a walk."

"Don't forget the locusts," Bert says. "Bears," I say. "Giant vampire bats."

Bert says he wants to tackle the challenge of crossing over the Shawangunks with me, so we bid adieu to the others and start the slow trudge up Route 44 into the rocky heart of Minnewaska State Park. I've driven this stretch many times before, but I've never had to walk it. It's slow going. We walk along the road for a couple of miles until we find the trailhead for Trapp's Trail; from there we follow switchbacks for eight miles, snaking out way closer to the top of the ridge. We pass some shaggy Billy goats who are surprised to see us. We're only about a mile from the top when we reach a clearing where there's someone from the power company standing there with an orange flag. "Sorry, rest of the trail is closed today," she says. "They're working on the power lines up ahead."

"You're kidding," I say, breathing hard from the climb.

"Not kidding," she says, smiling. "You'll have to go back."

"You don't understand," Bert says. "This guy here walked across the country."

Now she just looks confused. We continue to plead our case, but to no avail. It actually seems fitting for the last full day of this journey. Bert and I walk the three miles back down to the trailhead and call Mickey to come pick us up.

"Okay, I'll be right there."

An hour goes by and no sign of Mickey. Bert calls him again. "On my way," he says. "Where are you guys again?"

Finally we see Mickey's truck coming towards us. "What took you so long?"

"Wait a minute." I point to the corner of his mouth. "Is that mustard?"

"Maybe," he says. After a long pause, he breaks down. "Okay, listen. You guys called just when the brats came out of the kitchen. What am I supposed to do?"

Bert shakes his head. "Come pick us up?"

"These brats they've got, though," he says, making yummy sounds. "Just wait until you try these brats." In the future, the history books will refer to this moment as *The Mustard Incident*. Or at least, the guys sitting around the bar at the VFW will call it that.

Okay, turns out he's right: the brats at this place are indeed delicious. But I can't stay long because I've got the President's thing tonight. I'll see Mickey and Bert there, and I'll see the rest of the guys tomorrow when I get to the Walkway bridge. Right now, there's just enough time for me to grab a shower and a quick haircut before I head over to the Payne Mansion for a party that the President of Marist College is throwing in my honor and invited my parents, my aunts and uncles, my little brother John, Christa, and the whole gang from the VFW. Everyone is there.

Okay, almost everyone. Later tonight, President Murray will ask me *where is that beautiful fiancée of yours*, and I will tactfully change the subject.

POUGHKEEPSIE, NEW YORK

T HE LAST day of this epic Quest for the Holy Fail has finally come. I didn't sleep a wink last night at the mansion, but I admit I didn't really try – nope, I'm too jazzed up with a zillion memories from the past five months that want to swirl in my head like smoke before they leave. And I'm too restless struggling with the ten zillion possible answers to the one nagging question that doesn't want to leave me alone.

Namely, what the hell will I do when I wake up tomorrow?

On paper, today's walk is probably the closest I'll get to Easy Street all summer: only twelve miles, with a bit of a climb at the very start but smooth sailing the rest of the way on the flat, picturesque Hudson Valley Rail Trail. And I certainly won't have to walk this final stretch alone: today I have Christa and my little brother John to keep me company on this last leg, along with (drum roll, please) my very own Marist College security detail. Yes, President Murray is taking no chances on losing the big guy in the funny hat to a wrong turn or a sprained knee or a terrorist kidnapping before I reach the Marist campus, so he's assigned my very own body-guard, Ryan, who is actually a Marine Corps veteran as well as being a security guard at Marist. Thankfully, Ryan is a young guy with a great sense of humor about the whole deal, being assigned to birddog some homeless guy walking to campus at a breakneck pace of three miles per hour. For the record, I've never had a bodyguard before – well, other than my Mom on some early dates in high school – and I'm glad to have Ryan along for the ride, mainly because he seems to be the only one laughing at my corny jokes this morning. Christa just rolls her eyes as usual, and John's my younger brother, so he just takes out his ear pods, nods his head and says, "Uh huh. Yeah, man. Uh huh."

Oh, and speaking of company, let's not forget Marla has returned with a camera crew from *NBC Nightly News with Lester Holt*. They'll be following our little convoy all day in their TV truck, too. In fact, we're starting a half-hour late today because first, the NBC folks are having me walk this way and that on the back streets of New Paltz to get their required B-Roll footage. My feet still need their closeup. Julia is here at the start, biting her lip nervously and looking at her wristwatch every few minutes as I keep walking in circles for the NBC crew, burning daylight.

Finally, the NBC truck darts off to set up their gear farther down the route, and we start walking. I am restless to get underway. With Ryan keeping his distance behind us and constantly barking into his walkie-talkie, this feels like some kind of military operation. "*Pssht.* Go for Ryan ... Yes, on the move, on the move ... Corner of Main and Manheim ... Check that, Main and Pershall ... Roger that ... Ryan, out. *Pssht.*" After a couple of miles, I am half-expecting to hear a chopper hovering above, or at least a train of Humvees chugging alongside us as we march, with their bullhorns blaring out a warning to innocent bystanders on endless repeat, in multiple languages: *ATTENTION CITIZENS! STAY BACK, AND STAY CALM!*

I'm kidding, of course. And I know this much: I'm truly grateful for anybody caring enough to be out here walking the walk with me. But remember, all this sudden attention on the last day is quite shocking for a guy who's spent the last five months walking by himself.

What I don't know is, thanks to President Murray, the rest of the day is going to get a whole lot more shocking. For me, anyway.

First, a little bit of background on that. You might remember Dr. Murray calling my cell about a month ago in Wisconsin, to check in with one of his favorite faculty members and offer his best wishes on making it the rest of the way. And you might remember him telling me, back then, "We'll probably put together something on campus when you return. Something small, something simple. We'll focus on honoring our local veterans." Those were his exact words, as I recall: *something small, something simple.*

Okay, hold onto that thought for just a minute.

Christa and John are chatting away with one another as we walk, but I stay quiet. I guess I'm feeling torn: half of me can't wait to get home, and get back to my previous life. But the other half – the half that grew to actually enjoy living on the low road – wants to keep going. That half doesn't want the walk to end. That half even has ideas about turning around and going back, like Forrest Gump on endless repeat. I don't want to say this out loud, out of fear of Christa or John immediately whipping out their cell and calling for a doctor. But every step we take today, my anxiety about diving back into my previous life rises a little higher in my throat.

We hit the halfway mark and so far, the Rail Trail has been pretty empty; no vicious paparazzi hiding in the shadows, or at least, none that I can see. At one point, Ryan informs us our pace is actually a bit *too* fast, so we find a bench to take a break. Ryan stands apart on the pavement, chatting into his walkie-talkie. Two women are riding their bicycles past us the other way; they turn out to be a mother and daughter, out enjoying the fine day. The daughter abruptly stops and turns her bike around.

"Are you the walker guy?" she says, and we have a quick conversation before they ride on. She's actually a Marist student who just moved into her dorm on campus, and she had heard something about a professor walking across the country.

Ryan is still standing ten yards away, checking his phone, so naturally I have to berate his bodyguarding skills. Satirically, of course. "What happened, Ryan?" I say with as much fake anger as I can muster without breaking up. "Where was my security detail? I was fearing for my life. Those two women came out of *nowhere*."

"Sorry," he says, laughing. "It's my first time, guarding a celebrity."

Most of the walk today is along the Hudson Valley Rail Trail that extends from New Paltz to the Walkway Over the Hudson and into downtown Poughkeepsie. This used to be a working freight railway until the 1970s when the railway bridge burned down; then six years or so ago the bridge was rebuilt into a park. It's absolutely beautiful on a sunny day to stand on the Walkway so far above the shimmering Hudson.

There's a few hundred folks waiting for me as I close in on the Walkway that spans the Hudson River. Once we cross the Walkway, which is a little more than a mile in length itself, we take a sharp left down the stairs down onto Washington Street, heading straight for the Marist campus.

Okay, people. This is the part where Dr. Murray's *something small, something simple* line turns out to be a big, fat (and absolutely glorious) lie.

The first hint I get are the bagpipers who fall into formation in front of us as we walk. The second hint is the flotilla of fire trucks and first responder vehicles that fall into formation behind us. The streets of Poughkeepsie have been cleared all the way to campus.

The final hint – as if I needed another hint, at this point – is the thousands of people waiting ahead on the Marist campus as we get closer to the main gate, which is closed. We can hear them long before we can see them, shouting and cheering for what has turned out to be a hero's welcome.

Well played, President Murray. Well played. *Something small*, indeed.

Ryan is still barking into his radio as we close in on the enormous main gate at Marist. "We're a go for the gate opening. I repeat, we're a go for the gate."

I turn to Ryan. "Did you know about this?"

"Nope," he says, looking innocently up at the sky. "Above my pay grade." I turn to Christa. "Did you know about this?"

She laughs, shaking her head. "If I did, believe me, I would've brought something else to wear up on that stage."

My eyes get wider, if that's even possible. "There's a stage?"

She points ahead, and sure enough, past the slowly opening gates and throngs of students waiting behind them, I see a big stage set up in front of the Student Center. How big? Well, let's just say the Rolling Stones would feel comfortable up there, that's how big. "Holy cow," I say, genuinely frozen in fear the first time this whole summer. "What do I do, now?"

"You smile," Christa says, squeezing my hand. "And you keep walking."

Good advice from a great friend. When the massive iron gates swing open I imagine I've suddenly been dropped into that famous scene from *Willie Wonka and the Chocolate Factory*, where Gene Wilder opens the factory gates to greet the lucky ticket holders, surrounded by fanfare. Still in a trance, I manage to step forward to meet Dr. Murray and his wife, who are waiting for me on the stone path that leads into the beautiful Marist campus. I follow Dr. Murray onto the yellow brick road – or in this case, polished grey granite. Pretty much everything that happens next will become a bright blur in my memory; later I will view the pictures and videos from this amazing day, and in every one I will see the same glazed, overwhelmed look of surprise in my eyes.

But hey, at least I'm smiling.

It's difficult to describe that bright blur to folks who weren't there, without them rolling their eyes and immediately thinking, *you must be exaggerating. You must be making this all up.* But if you were there, then you know exactly what I'm talking about.

The Marist Band played. The Marist singers sang. The Amerscot bagpipers marched back and forth, piping the whole way. A giant cannon manned by Civil War reenactors went off every few minutes with an echoing boom, and they were joined by Abraham Lincoln himself, or at least, someone dressed like Honest Abe, working the crowd like he was running for re-election. There were dozens of my fellow veterans from the VFW joining me on the stage, Mickey and Bert included. All total there must have been five thousand people on campus that day, everyone cheering and shouting their support. It was so loud, I remember being frightened to the point where I almost wanted to disappear, maybe duck into a restroom or utility closer to escape the noise after spending all that time on the low road, quiet and alone.

It feels like a rally to welcome home a hero. Which is probably why I'm so shocked, because I don't feel like a hero at all.

As I approach the stage, I receive perhaps the biggest (and most pleasant) surprise of the entire day: there's my friend Doris in the front row, my favorite guardian angel, in a wheelchair waving an American flag. With her giant atlas, she's told me where I was walking the whole summer, but the last time we talked on the phone she was the one having trouble walking, so she was probably the last person I'd expect to show. "You're here," I say, bending down to give her a gentle hug.

"Are you kidding? Honey, I wouldn't miss this for the world," she says. "Now get on up there."

Christa and I sit next to one another on the stage, the guys from the VFW standing in a row behind us, and we whisper to each other just how humbling it is to be in the spotlight of this whole grand spectacle. There's a long list of speeches by local dignitaries including Christa, followed by President Murray himself. My legs feel weak, and I can barely stand when he asks me to come up to the podium and speak. Ironically, after all those miles on the road, I need to lean on my walking stick the most today, after the walk is over.

Folks, I wish I could tell you exactly what I said on the podium that day, but to be honest I can't recall much. I will always remember two things: first, apologizing to Dr. Murray and all the students present, because I only had two days to get ready for the fall semester and I couldn't even remember my Marist passwords to log onto my office computer. Talk about out of the frying pan and into the fire.

"Does anyone here have me for a class this semester?" I say to the thousands of students in front of me, most wearing their Marist red & white with pride. Everyone laughs, and more than a few students raise their hands.

"Forgive me," I tell them. "But this first week of class is going to be a little rough." The second thing I will always remember from that blur of a day is the very last thing I said at the podium. It's something that will resonate with me long after the smoke clears from this amazing adventure, and I'm so lucky I managed to say something this profound while in my state of utter shock.

"The walk might be over," I say. "But the journey is just beginning."

For such a long and epic poem, the ending of Homer's *Odyssey* is very abrupt. After our hero returns home to slay the suitors and regain his family, the blood on his sword hasn't even had time to dry before the curtain falls. We're not given any details about how Odysseus lives the rest of his life, so we have to assume he does indeed carry the winnowing oar inland, as the oracle foretold, to officially end his quest and find his fate in blissful retirement. We must imagine him happy, it seems, growing old gracefully as king of Ithaca during a long period of peace, his wife Penelope and son Telemachus dutifully at his side. Now that his adventure is over, we assume Odysseus will hang up his shield and walking stick for good, content with daily strolls along the beach and perhaps discovering a harmless hobby in these twilight years, like canning peaches or manicuring those tiny trees, until he finally dies a gentle death of old age, his younger days of high adventure only a distant memory.

Well, that's clearly bullshit.

It doesn't work like that. Take it from a guy who just walked across the country: when you complete an epic journey, you don't want to stop. The passion you earned during that quest doesn't simply disappear, or fade away. It stays with you. You can't turn it off. Yes, it is a blessing having such an intense fire burning inside your chest, but it's also a curse, because the fire never goes out, even after the story ends. Instead, it keeps building, pushing you to want to do even more, even though the quest is long over. That's what happened for me at the end of my own adventure. When Edward Payson Weston finally reached San Francisco in 1907, his first instinct was to keep going, too; reports mentioned the old man wanted to keep walking all the way to Canada or Mexico or even back to New York. So I imagine that's exactly what happened for our hero Odysseus, as well. I can't see him being satisfied and happy at the end of his story, ready for some fuzzy slippers and long snoozes in a cozy chair. No, I imagine him restless and moody, still filled with the same smoldering fire he once needed to defeat the Cyclops and the Sirens but not quite sure what to do with it, hoping the day will come when he can rip his walking stick off the wall, step outside his door, and do it all over again.

EXIT WOUNDS

AUGUST 23, 2020

A<small>ND THERE</small> you have it. It's been exactly one year to the day
since I walked – okay, maybe *stumbled* would be a better
verb choice – onto the Marist College campus in a daze to put an
end the VetZero Walk Across America. Normally a year goes by
pretty fast, especially when you've reached a certain grey age, like
me; but with most of 2020 covered in a treacherous fog of COVID
and various other disasters, I think you'll agree last summer
already feels more than a few worlds away. The current pandemic
has provided us daily grim reminders that our lives are short and
mostly unpredictable. It's been difficult to find any silver linings
in our lives for as long as we can remember, it seems – but at least
all this social distancing has afforded me one positive side effect:
there's been a lot of down time to process my adventure last summer, and try to find some answers to those big questions I asked
myself before we started. One thing's for sure: the life lessons of
perseverance and adjustment I learned on the low road seem even
more important now, as we all try adjust to our "new normal" and
persevere through the monumental health crisis that's ruined our
whole year.

So in my case, I guess hindsight is indeed 2020.

When I got back last summer, a lot of people told me, "You

must be so happy to sleep in your own bed again." Others said, "You must be glad to have things back to normal." But there was a big problem: after five months living on the road, I wasn't sure what my normal was any more. So I had a hard time readjusting back to the routines of my old life, once the walk ended. I had trouble sleeping in my own bed, or any bed really; I ended up sprawled on the couch or even curled up on the floor in a sleeping bag more times than I could count. For months I would wake up in the middle of the night, eyes wide with worry, unable to fall back asleep. And when I did manage to sleep, I'd wake up with these horrible leg cramps, my calves or hamstrings suddenly seizing up without warning, leaving me whimpering in the dark as I waited for the stabbing pain to subside.

I also had trouble dealing with crowds and loud noises; for the first few months, I found myself ducking out of social events because I couldn't handle being surrounded by a lot of people, or a lot of voices. For a social person like myself, this was a huge change. I felt overwhelmed even before I walked into a crowded room; that autumn, I remember being honored by a standing ovation from hundreds of my faculty colleagues at our first faculty plenary. It was a touching moment, but I could barely manage a smile because secretly my heart was racing a mile a minute with anxiety. Thankfully one of my colleagues in Psychology recognized my anxiety that day, and talking with her was a great help. And I'd feel that anxiety even in smaller settings, or whenever people would come up to me wanting to talk about the walk. After only a few seconds, I would avert their eyes, already looking for an exit.

That newfound anxiety really surprised me, but the most sobering part is this: I was only living out there for about five months. I can't imagine what that withdrawal must feel like for a veteran who has been homeless for years, or even worse, most of their adult lives. Yet, we know there are over 40,000 veterans living on the street each and every night in America, having the same problems adjusting to a society that seems to pass them by, day after day.

I also had a lot of difficulty with my job when I returned to Marist for the fall semester. I struggled mightily with the normal deadlines, conference calls, office hours, department meetings and all the other routine duties I used to breeze through after twenty years as a college professor. Weirdly, I felt like I was learning everything for the first time. I still find myself zoning out in faculty meetings when folks drone on about the usual this and that; I catch myself looking out the window. I want to stand up in the middle of the meeting and shout, *Nothing we're doing here is going to change the world, people. None of this is making the world a better place.* I want to jump out of my cushioned chair, bang the conference table with my fist and cry out, *Let's start walking the walk, and stop talking the talk! Who's with me?*

But I won't. Nothing says restraining order faster than a burly middle-aged guy busting up the furniture, of course. But it's not all bad here at Marist. On the bright side, that passion has given me a renewed energy towards my students. More than ever before, I want to help them discover their own personal passion, and I want to give them the confidence to realize they can actually do something about it. I don't know if that makes me a better teacher or not; it definitely makes me a more passionate one. But I really don't have a choice in the matter; thanks to the walk, this is who I am now, and I don't see myself changing back to the old Tommy anytime soon.

It's been a year, but I still have plenty of physical reminders about the walk, every single day. My knees are still wobbly and I can't walk down stairs. Standing up from a chair or getting out of a car is always a minor embarrassment. Sometimes my feet swell up like balloons just because it's Tuesday, and sometimes my knees refuse to bend, altogether. As a result, whatever fitness I achieved last summer has quickly been erased; a couple months ago, I decided to walk another 22 miles in a day to raise money for VetZero. I made it – but barely. This time around, there wasn't a crowd of thousands as I limped to the finish line, or a Civil War cannon, or Abraham Lincoln. It was just me, and to be honest it felt good doing the 22 miles without anyone watching. Well, actually there was one person waiting: good old Mickey, sitting on the steps in front of the VFW as I hobbled the last few yards. He's juggling a cold bottle of water in his hands.

"You look horrible," he says, shaking his head like a high school coach trying to tell a kid there's no way in hell he's making this team.

"Thanks," I moan, flopping down on the ground. "Trust me, I feel worse."

"Exactly," he says, handing me the water.

When I stood up on that podium at Marist, I said the walk was over, but the journey had just begun. And boy, was I right. I definitely got to enjoy my fifteen minutes of fame: there was a good stretch of time after I got home when I couldn't pay for my own coffee anywhere around here. I received proclamations, certificates and plaques from just about every elected leader in the tri-state area, including a medal from Governor Cuomo. I also got the chance to speak before the New York State Assembly on veterans' mental health issues. Dutchess County added an emergency fund for local veterans-in-need to the annual budget, and its official name is the *Tommy Zurhellen Fund.* How cool is that? I write a biweekly column about veterans in the local paper, and I still join Boris & Robyn on WPDH every Wednesday morning to talk about veterans' issues on the *Commander Tom Report*, where I even get my own theme music! And speaking of music, I can even say walking across the country allowed me to play Carnegie Hall. No, really! Well, to be completely honest, I was invited to MC the annual Veterans Day concert at Carnegie Hall last November, where I introduced the different pieces of music and told the audience a little about my walk. (Okay, so technically I didn't play an instrument, but I did manage to bang the big drum a few times in rehearsals, so I'm sticking with my story.) Seriously though, I'm still pinching myself to make sure I wasn't dreaming of standing on the same stage where everyone from Groucho Marx and Aretha Franklin to The Beatles once stood. That was one of the most humbling moments of my life, and I know I'll never forget it.

And that's just the stuff I can remember off the top of my head. But after a few short months all that glory faded, of course, and now I pay for my own coffee again. I'm still Commander of the Poughkeepsie VFW, and that work I started doing to help local vets back before the walk has grown exponentially into a full-time job. We put together 500 more of those VetZero backpacks this past winter, and just this summer alone, we've made and delivered over 1,000 meals for our neighbors in need during the pandemic. Christa and I still find time to grab a socially-distanced beer and dream up ways to do more for our local vets. For example, we used some of the money we raised from the walk to start a VetZero Ride program which gives local veterans a free ride to any essential appointments – doctor, lab tests, job interview, you name it – and it's been quite a success so far. The car itself is all tricked out in the green and black VetZero logo, and every time I see it whizzing around town, I get really happy. I think to myself, *hey, I helped make that.* Every time I see it driving by in the opposite direction, it's a reminder that I've done something small to make the world a better place. It's regular proof to me that one person can indeed make a difference.

Christa and I actually watched the VetZero Ride zoom by just the other day; we were sitting outside in downtown Poughkeepsie, enjoying our regular, weekday, socially-distanced cold beer in the late summer sun. Hey, now that I think about it, this would actually be the perfect scene to end the book, wouldn't it? Perfect! I love it when a story comes together, and comes full circle. All we need now is the two main protagonists to say something pithy to one another and we can wrap up the whole book – luckily, Christa and I say pithy things all the time, with or without the beer. And hey, while we're at it, let's blast Journey's "Don't Stop Believin'" behind them, as the screen slowly dissolves to black. "Do you ever think about doing it again?" Christa says. "The walk, I mean."

"Not today," I say, rubbing my aching knees. "But never say never, I guess." And ... *cut*. Print it. That's a wrap, people!

Stay tuned for the rushed, inevitable sequel called *The Low Road 2: The Final Frontier* where Tommy puts on a spacesuit and tries to walk all the way to the Moon!

Okay, not so fast. I've just been informed that I can't finish this book without sharing some of the lessons I learned last summer while walking across America alone. Turns out the whole reason people read memoirs, I'm being told, is to live vicariously through someone else's adventures and learn to walk a mile in their shoes, so we can apply the important lessons they learned to our own lives. Okay, fair enough. At the start of this whole story I remember saying I didn't want to write a self-help book, and that's still true. What I really wanted to write was a book that gave other folks the confidence or courage or general, all-around, American chutzpah to take a chance on their own quixotic adventure to make the world a better place. I hope I've done that, but who knows. I guess the only way to be sure will come one day in the future, when I go to the mailbox and I find a sparkling new copy of *your* book waiting for me. So will you please get on that, already? (Seriously, I can't wait to read it.)

The truth is, I feel like I learned enough last summer to fill three or four memoirs, let alone just one. Every day I spent out there on the low road was an education. Every time I talked with a veteran, I walked away with another lesson. Every day turned out to be completely different, and that's a big reason why I kept going. None of it was easy, but looking back now, I wouldn't trade any of the lessons I learned for all the Nutter Butters in the world.

Here are some of those lessons I will never forget.

I learned it's really expensive to be homeless in America. When you're living on the road or the streets, there's no place to store your food, and obviously, no place to cook it. I ended up buying each meal individually, and I was forced to buy them at gas stations and convenience stores where access to fresh food is limited and prices are premium. I ate a lot of junk food; I can't count the nights I had to settle on a bag of Corn Nuts, a Snickers Bar and a big jug of Gatorade, just for the calories. Those three items alone cost me ten bucks at a gas station. Being homeless is expensive in other ways, too; it taxes your soul. I had to depend on the kindness of strangers for almost everything at one time or another, even going to the bathroom. When you are homeless, you depend on others for your basic human dignity, and that is something no American should have to experience. It's safe to say, I will never take all the good things in my life for granted, ever again.

I learned veterans don't share their stories with just anyone. To so many of our veterans, stories are sacred; the good ones are tucked away in the dark, written in a secret code most of us can't decipher. But when veterans talk to other veterans, those stories come out because even though all veterans are different, they all speak the same, secret language. I listened as dozens of veterans all across America told me their stories, because they trusted me with their secrets. I saw a lot of amazing sights on my walk – including the ramp my childhood hero Evel Knievel used to (almost) jump across Snake Canyon, holy cow! – but none of them compare to the thrill I got from listening to veterans tell me their stories. That's the good part. But there's a bad part, too, about veterans keeping their stories close to the vest; no matter what, they don't want to talk about their problems, with doctors or anyone else. There's a real stigma among veterans that sharing is a sign of weakness. In the service, you don't talk about your problems, and if you do, you get marked as a complainer, or worse. I've learned that in order to help our heroes overcome mental health issues, we have to somehow overcome that stigma that prevents them from opening up. I also learned that having those veterans in crisis talk to other veterans is a great first step. I've seen that connection work, time and again. The outstanding *Vet 2 Vet* program we have in Poughkeepsie is just that: veterans talking to veterans. It sounds simple, but it works, and I think we need to do much more of that.

In addition, I learned we're not doing enough to support veterans in this country. Everyone might automatically say, "Thank you for your service." That gesture might make us feel better about how we treat out veterans in this country, but it doesn't do much to help veterans. Most of the folks I met on my walk were genuinely surprised about the numbers of 22 veteran suicides each day in America, and over 40,000 homeless veterans in America each night. Doing right by our military veterans is probably the only issue we can all agree on, and yet, we are not educated on the grim realities many of our heroes face, each and every day. The VA can do more, sure, but it can't possibly do everything; the answer has to come from all of us, in every community and neighborhood. We all need to do a better job. That job starts with continuing to raise awareness about the 22 and the 40,000 in America, until every single citizen realizes what's at stake.

And I'm optimistic about that, because my journey also taught me America is filled with a lot more kindness than hate. True story. These days, we are told we live in an angry world. Turn on the news: every time we walk out our door we're warned to watch out for bad weather, bad neighborhoods, bad critters (murder hornets!) and bad people. And yet, I didn't see any of that in the

America I walked through last summer. Listen, I walked alone through the most rural places in America like the high deserts of Wyoming and Oregon, and I also walked alone through struggling cities like Flint, Buffalo, and Milwaukee. Not once did I ever feel unwelcome, threatened, or in danger. On the contrary, every conversation I had with complete strangers was about kindness. Every time I met someone new I could feel genuine empathy and caring. The worst thing to happen to me after walking 2,800 miles through every part of America was having my walking stick stolen. Yes, I realize I have an inherent advantage in walking across America being a (very) large, white male; I know a woman or a person of color attempting the same journey would no doubt have a much different experience. I fully acknowledge that. But I still want to share that all my personal fears about the America I would encounter were unfounded. I was surprised by so much love at every turn.

I learned so much about myself. I discovered I had a lot of compassion, patience, emotional energy and empathy hidden inside, just waiting to get out. I learned I'm a lot stronger than I thought, too. At least on the inside. After my walk, I know for certain there are things in my life I will never take for granted again. I also know I've gained a true passion for helping veterans in need, and that passion probably isn't going to fade anytime soon. It feels like a calling, and that calling is only getting stronger every day. I learned to take a risk on the low road; like the poet said, "I took the one less traveled by / and that has made all the difference."

In the end, I learned to love the low road. Along the way, somehow, I learned to love myself a little more, too. And now I'm convinced the only way to see America is at three miles per hour. I hope you feel the same way I do.

But what about the one question that started this whole Quest for the Holy Fail, you may ask? I've sure had enough time to think about it, with more than a year gone by. Did I ever get closer to answering the question that pushed me onto the low road in the first place?

Namely, can one person change the world?

My answer might surprise you. I know it sure surprised me! After all, I was the guy who walked across America without support vehicles or an entourage or anything like that; it was just me, an underprepared guy with a backpack stumbling to find his own way. I couldn't have been *more* alone last summer, I think. But I definitely did not do it alone. Sure, I might have been walking alone, but I never would have made it without the constant support, love and inspiration from so many other people. No one would have ever heard the big guy in a funny hat if it wasn't for Nora and Julia at Marist working hard every day to share our story. And I wouldn't have walked far at all if folks like Paul, Jeff, Tim, James and dozens of others who kept me going on the road. The way I see it, the walk belongs as much to the thousands of folks who shared and donated on Facebook over the summer as it does to me. Together, we raised over $60,000 to help veterans in Poughkeepsie. I can't take credit for that. And together, we got to share our story with over 12 million Americans through *NBC Nightly News*, *Fox News*, the *New York Post*, dozens of local TV stations and newspapers across the country, and dozens more social media sites. I can't take credit for that, either. And now that I think about it, I can't name one thing about last summer that I did all by myself. There was always someone else, helping, hoping, supporting.

So, can one person truly make a difference in the world? No. I believe you make a difference by sparking passion in others to light their own way, and in turn, they do it for others, and so on, until you have an honest-to-God movement on your hands. If you simply try to go it by yourself, you might be filling your own ego, but you won't get very far. That's the secret. The late, great Justice Ruth Bader Ginsburg knew that when she said, "Fight for the things you care about, but do it in a way that will lead others to join you." She knew you can't go it alone. You have to let people in, and you have to rely on other people's passion to really make a change. All you really can do is try to be that spark for others, and hope the fire spreads far and wide enough to make the change you're hoping for. You won't get credit for it, but that's not why you're doing it in the first place. Right? Fact: there's around 12 million more folks out there who know about the challenges of veterans' mental health and homelessness in America, thanks to the VetZero Walk Across America. That impact still boggles my mind. But I would be an absolute fool to believe I did that, all by myself.

Actually, I'm betting the biggest impact is still to come, because I hope you read this book and it sparks something inside of you, to try to make a real difference in your own world. I hope reading my story has given you a little boost of confidence to follow your own passion, and your own foolhardy adventures. Trust me, you've got this. I look forward to reading all about your own Quest. And I'll be sure to look for you – where else? – out there on the low road.

AFTER/WORDS

Cheryl Strayed's amazing memoir *Wild* chronicled her solo journey along the Pacific Crest Trail, and it was a huge inspiration for me as I wrote my own book about a solo journey into the unknown. But my favorite element of *Wild* isn't the *solo* part; no, it's the endless variety of interesting characters she meets on and off the trail. When I finished her book, I immediately wanted to know more about these folks. I wanted to hear more about their own stories, in their own voices. How did they feel when they encountered Cheryl on the trail? What were they doing before that encounter, and what did they do after? Did they even agree with her account of events that appear in the book?

As a result, I knew I wanted to include the unfiltered voices of the amazing people I met while walking across America in *The Low Road*. So in this final section of the book, I've invited all the folks from the previous pages to share their own perspectives, in their own words. Some responded to my invitation, and others did not. Thank you so much to all the folks who took the time to write down or record their impressions of our time together last summer. I've arranged their commentaries loosely in chronological order, starting with Boris, the local radio DJ in Poughkeepsie from *The Boris & Robyn Show* who gave me my very first break at sharing my story, even before the walk began.

I hope you will enjoy listening to their voices as much as I have!

BORIS

The first time I met "Commander Tom" was when he walked into our WPDH studio to be interviewed on the *Boris & Robyn Morning Show* about some crazy idea to walk across America. Standing in the shadow of this huge, hulking man for the first time, my co-host Robyn and I just stared at each other, thinking the same thing: "There's *no way* this guy is going to be able to walk from Oregon to New York." But each week as we talked to Tom on-air from the road, we quickly realized just how much spirit and determination he had. Not a day went by during the summer of 2019 when I wasn't thinking about where Tom was and what he was doing.

When I was at the beach, Tom was walking.

When I was out for lunch with friends, Tom was walking.

When I was napping comfortably at home in the AC, Tom was still walking.

I wasn't haunted just with the thought this foolish man who was slowly making his way back to Poughkeepsie, but of the lives of all the homeless veterans that Tom was walking for every day. That summer, while my life went on as usual, Tom was roughing it. And so were more than 40,000 homeless veterans who, unlike Commander Tom, don't have a place to eventually come home to. That summer my eyes were opened, not only to what a genuinely inspirational person Tom is, but to the reality that so much more needs to be done for our veteran population.

NORA

The big question on my mind during spring of Senior Year at Marist College was: would I be employed? Like every other graduating senior, I was focused on the "what's next" of life after college. The uncertainty was overwhelming at times, but I was grateful for my job in the Marketing Department at Marist College during the school year. It kept me active and creative. One day I wandered into the office to meet with my boss, Brian. When I entered, he was staring at some papers in his hands. He looked up at me and welcomed me with, "Do you know Professor Tommy Zurhellen?"

"Yes, I'm an English major," I replied.

"Well," he said, looking up at me. "He is walking across the country."

I'm sure like every other response Tommy had been getting, the only thing that came to mind was, "Huh?" Brian explained the VetZero mission, and that Tommy needed a social media intern for the summer to keep everyone updated on his journey and help fundraise. I was hesitant at first; could I handle an internship and potentially a full-time job at the same time? I read over the papers Brian had given me and the route Tommy planned to take. I couldn't believe it to be honest, but I was too intrigued by the journey.

Of course I said, "I'll do it."

One of my favorite parts of the summer was witnessing the kindness of people. The generosity of people was astounding. The VetZero Facebook page was flooded with messages every day, "What can I do to help?" People across the country were hearing about Tommy's journey and they wanted to pitch in. People offered up money, gift cards, food, their homes, etc. With each update from Tommy came a flood of notifications with comments of encouragement and motivation. When our t-shirt campaign launched, I was hoping to sell at least 50 shirts, we ended up selling over 150+ shirts! I wore my t-shirt all summer with pride and gladly explained the mission to anyone who asked.

In June, I was invited to NY Cub Scout Troop 33's crossover ceremony and summer BBQ. They had raised money for VetZero and created a plethora of handwritten notes and cards to send to Tommy. I was nervous at first showing up on my own with a camera in hand, but everyone welcomed me immediately. The cub scouts showed me pictures of their family members who were veterans, told me stories, and asked questions about Tommy. Every person I spoke to had a sparkle in their eye and a gasp at the end of each sentence. "Wow, he's really doing it."

The next day, one of Tommy's friends named Jennifer set up a fundraiser at the local Outback Steakhouse, with all the proceeds going to the VetZero mission. I didn't know what to expect when I arrived with my brother, but I was greeted with a big hug from Jennifer. She had created posters and had them standing in front of the restaurant. She stopped everyone that came in and explained the special lunch event happening for the day. She spoke with such passion and pointed to every photo on the board. The local Stop & Shop had donated two sheet cakes with VetZero written across them in VetZero Kelly Green icing. As I chowed down on some wings, Tommy facetimed me. I "walked him" over to the table full of people from his VFW. They were so excited to see him! You could tell how much they respected him, and this mission, and how grateful they were to get to see his face, even if just for a moment. As I hung up and joined my brother back at our table, I couldn't help but feel a little guilty. I was in a cool restaurant on a summer's day enjoying a yummy meal, and Tommy was in the middle of the country wondering where his next meal would be, or where he'd lay to rest that night.

This is the harsh reality of too many of our veterans in this country. I realized how privileged I was not to have to worry about the basic necessities of life. The first step is recognizing the privilege, the next step I told myself was: what do I do with this now? How can I do more?

The fall after my VetZero internship I went to a festival on Long Island with some friends. It was set up along the water on the North Shore of Long Island where local restaurants, vendors, and artisans came together for a large street fair. As we walked down the street browsing the local tents, I noticed an older gentleman ahead of us, in the middle of the street. He was wearing a VFW hat and a uniform. Across from him I noticed the VFW tent set up with a young lady sitting at a table. The older gentleman was trying to stop people and get their attention, but everyone walked right past, not even making eye contact. Admittedly before my internship with VetZero I probably would've done the same. But I walked right up to him and introduced myself. He explained to me they were raising money for the local VFW. In true millennial fashion I didn't have much cash on me, but I gave him whatever I had. He led me over to the table, and I explained my summer internship to him. He couldn't believe the story, but he was smiling from ear to ear while I told it. He gave me a Poppy pin and said, "For you Nora, you made my day."

Although I may never have the courage to walk across the country like Tommy did, the most important lesson I learned is that little changes can make a big difference. Stopping to speak with a veteran about the local VFW and donating what I could made a small change.

On my lunch break at work on the Fourth of July I wandered down main street admiring the "Hometown Heroes" signs they had posted on the light poles. I took the time to look at each face and read each name. On a street I drove past every day, I now noticed the building on the corner was our own local VFW. If we all stopped to pay attention, we could change our veterans' lives. It starts by taking that pause, listening to their stories, then acting. I am so glad I accepted this internship and was able to play a small role in this incredible mission. I am also so grateful for all the lessons I learned along the way. The mission's never over, and I am proud to have this newfound awareness for veterans, the struggles they face, and the help they need.

And I know Tommy will never stop, either! The day he arrived back in Poughkeepsie, he turned to me and said, "So, are you around next summer?"

COACH PETE

When a mutual acquaintance suggested a meeting back in March 2019 with English professor Tommy Zurhellen, a colleague and now friend at Marist College, I was excited at the idea. Several of my former and current runners had spoken highly of him – college students getting jacked up about an English professor and talking about it at track practice ... that's kind of rare. And besides, his idea of walking 22 miles a day across the USA was intriguing as hell to me. We connected via email and he suggested a meeting at Starbucks across the street from Marist. (In hindsight, I wish I had the guts to tell him how much I despise Starbucks.) And then, I catch a quick glimpse of Tommy, first time I'm meeting him, at friggin' *Starbucks*, and I see this big hulking presence of a man, shaped not unlike an upright freezer, and I think to myself: "How the f*ck is THIS dude gonna walk across the country?" I sat down with him, we chatted for a bit, he tells me he did a practice walk from rural Amenia to his home in the City of Poughkeepsie – 22 miles across Dutchess County – and I'm still not impressed. Ambling across an average size county in upstate New York is not the same as walking across the country, 22 miles, every damn day, for months at a time! Would I provide him some coaching advice along the way, Tommy asked? You know, tips for hydration, changing walking shoes and socks, motivational messages, stuff like that ... and it would be posted on Facebook, to promote the walk. Sure, sure, I said, still incredulous that this big dude could pull it off.

Here's the thing: The more I got to know Tommy, the more convinced I was that the big man would be up to the big task. We stayed in touch throughout the spring and summer. I told my jogging buddies, my wife, my friends, anyone who would listen (or not!) about his walk. Even bought me one of them cool "Vet Zero" shirts and proudly marched in the Memorial Day and Fourth of July parades in Hyde Park with it on. I was a fan, a believer, a convert. With every post on Facebook and every day he inched closer to home, I realized this guy was a great role model for overcoming physical challenges with the proper mindset. That big dude I met in Starbucks? He proved to be up to the task. And when the big man ambled across campus on that warm August day in 2019 at the end of the walk, I was a proud coach, honored to have played a tiny part in his big and important project. Tommy's journey hasn't concluded after all those months and all those miles in the summer of 2019. He still does a ton of great things for the veterans of Dutchess County -- men and women who served this country honorably and proudly. Marist College, and the greater Poughkeepsie community, is lucky to have him. I raise my Stewart's (not Starbucks!) cup to him. Then, and now.

Way to go, hombre.

MICKEY

Actually, I first heard about the walk from my brother, of all people. He called me from South Dakota and said, "Hey Mick, somebody from your VFW Post in Poughkeepsie is walking across the country." And I said no way, nobody here is *that* crazy. But I thought if anyone was that crazy, it would be my friend Tom. And I was right.

When we did talk, do you remember the first thing I said to you? Exactly. I said, "You're crazy."

Listen, I did the Bataan death march thing in the New Mexico desert, and I did a bunch of other walks back in the day, so I know just how crazy you are. But when you started the walk, I also supported you every step of the way.

Me and Bert came out to walk the last couple days with you. The first day was a mistake: uphill the whole way, raining, tractor trailers flying by us the whole time.

The second day was better, sunny, and we had some other guys from the VFW walking with us. But I know you want me to talk about the Mustard Incident, so I'm going to tell my side of the story. Here goes.

That day, Tom and Bert were walking the last leg over the Shawangunk mountain while I took the truck over the mountain to the Brau Haus to wait for them on the other side, where we would all have some brats and beers together to put a nice cap on the day. We knew it would be a few more hours before we saw those guys, so we ended up ordering lunch. Okay, it was an early lunch. As soon as we order, the phone call comes in from Bert and Tom: come pick us up, we're done. And then I said, okay we're on our way! And I hung up.

Well, when I said "on our way," I meant, *after* we finish our food, and these big German beers. Then we'll be on our way. Okay? That's what I meant.

So we came and picked you guys up like an hour later. Okay, maybe an hour and a half. And you said, "Did you guys stop? What took you so long?"

I denied everything. I said, "You hear that? That's my stomach growling, okay? We didn't eat nothing."

But then you saw the mustard on my moustache and you called me on it.

As I remember, then you got real angry. So I got angry too, and two miles before the Brau Haus I kicked you out of the truck, with your walking stick, and I said, "You're on a walk across the country, then you gotta finish the walk. Get out, we'll wait for you down below."

You showed up an hour later, cooled off, and we had a good time.

The next day was the final day, and me and the other VFW guys waited for you at the beginning of the Walkway. Then we drove over and met you at Marist. They had a big ceremony there, NBC News, there was a cannon, everything. We all stood up on stage, the VFW guys. One of the guys passed out because he locked his knees, and he says, "Mike, I'm going down," so I caught him. All the students were there, had to be 5,000 people there at Marist. It was quite a day.

Later, my son who lives in South Dakota calls me all excited and says, "Dad, Dad, I saw you on the TV, on *NBC Nightly News*. In South Dakota!" Now I was famous, too.

You did quite an accomplishment, Commander. But I still think you're crazy.

PAUL

Brother, when you first called, I thought the idea was a bit ... *far-fetched*. Okay, more than a bit. I loved the thought and meaning behind the cause, but it was a big undertaking and let's face it, you might have bitten off more then you could chew. At the same time, you know I was more than willing to help out as much as I could. When you showed up at the airport in Portland I was just so happy to see you, as it had been far too many years. Then I thought, I guess this is real and it's happening and was just very proud of you and also concerned for you as it was going to be quite a feat. The next day during our walk together on Day One, I really felt inspired. Talking to those other veterans along the way was very eye-opening for me. They all loved hearing what you were doing, and they were all so moved. I was proud to have been a part of it, and at the same time a bit ashamed of myself for not doing more to help. After the walk that day I was tired and sore and worried for my friend with so many miles to go. But more importantly I was just inspired by the cause. Thank you, Tommy, for reminding me (and so many others) that one person can make a difference.

BAKER

Tommy Z is one of those rare friends where it always clicks right away, no matter how long it's been.

When I met up with Tommy and some fellow veterans at a bar called the Dutch Goose on State Street in Boise, they'd just walked nine miles in from the suburbs to Veterans Park -- a light day for Tommy, but the other guys were wiped out and everyone was glad for the beers in front of them. When I walked in they all welcomed me, Tommy gave me one of his bear hugs, we bickered over who was paying for the next round (Tommy won), and *bam*, we were back.

The old jokes from grad school came rolling: General Tso's tofu killers, the Shiner, and--for reasons neither of us can remember-- the phrase "You're in *faaaaaaaaat city!*" And I heard all about Tommy's early trials on the trail—he had all the wrong gear, he almost froze to death, his ankles were brittle as glass. And of course, the mountain lions.

At his last mail stop he'd received something like forty packs of Nutter Butters, but what he really needed was the right gear.

That night he came to stay at our house in Boise. We showed him around our new town, and I had a good time goofing off with my kids and an old friend. That evening my wife and I insisted Tommy take our big, comfy king-size bed to get a good rest, and we bickered as he said the couch would be fine (this time, I won).

Very early that next morning I drove Tommy out to the edge of town to pick up the trail he'd found. At the exit, we went maybe fifty yards, and on the right I saw a store named, of all things, *Fat City Fireworks*.

It felt like kismet that Tommy was going to have a great day. Of course, I was wrong. "You're in *faaaaaaaat city*!" I quipped.

But Tommy wasn't listening. He was looking out the other way at a grassy field. "Where's the trail? There's supposed to be a trail here," he said. He got out, shouldered his fat backpack, and said, "Well, thanks for everything, brother. Wish me luck."

CHRIS

My name is Chris and I served in the United States Marine Corps, with multiple deployments in Afghanistan. I first met Tommy when I was working for the local taxi company in Mountain Home, Idaho. He needed a ride into town to refill water and rest a twisted ankle. When I had picked him up from the side of the road I kind of recognized him but wasn't sure. We started making small talk. When I asked him why he was out here walking, he informed me that he was trekking across the country. This reminded me of a story that I had read a couple weeks back about an individual walking across the country for veteran suicide.

He then laughed a little and said, "Yeah, that's me."

We then talked a bit before getting to the gas station where I got his information and the information for VetZero. After leaving the station to go back to work I started thinking: I contacted a group that I rode with as well as the local bars and people I knew. Here in Mountain Home, veterans are loved as well as respected. The town has a yearly parade for the Air Force where they even get jets to do fly-bys from the base right outside of town. Once I got the word out people started donating money to help Tommy get any supplies he needed. I even had the manager of a local hotel offer him a room for free, which was good because the one he had picked out was not the best in town. After a few hours I gathered everything that was donated and found out which room he was staying in and surprised him. He was almost speechless and had a grin from ear to ear knowing that people had come together so quickly for such an amazing cause. I have very strong feelings towards people like Tommy and organizations such as VetZero, and I absolutely love what they do.

In my personal experience I have struggled with suicide and depression, not only in myself but a lot of my fellow Marines I served with but a lot of friends and veterans I have spent time with. This man did something absolutely amazing for a cause very close to my heart and I have the utmost respect for Tommy Zurhellen and am extremely thankful that there are wonderful people like this working every day to help those that have served.

CARL

As I drove through the early season snow, I pondered the fella I was about to meet. My high school pal Paul had posted about his Navy buddy who was walking across country to raise awareness for the 22 veterans on average who take their own lives every day. I decided to take the old VW camper up into Wyoming and play a support role, as I had never served and this guy was walking across some of the most unpopulated land in our country. I kept thinking, man, the backpack and all those supplies must be backbreaking.

When I pulled up to the meeting spot, a big fella came out, hopped in and shut the door. Where's your pack? Never mind, I'll ask later, let's go get on with dinner. Clearly exhausted and a bit disoriented even, Tommy politely sat up with me a while after dinner for a few beers and even a taste of Wyoming whisky. Clearly the campfire was comforting but I could tell the bed in the camper was calling.

Over breakfast I began asking about some of the things that I was curious about. Where's all your gear? Don't you have a cooking stove or a coffee press? Nope, this maniac was traveling light ... like, insane person light. I knew he had a mail pickup the night before to resupply. Okay, so where's all *that* stuff? Well, Tommy simply had found an old folks' home, and donated most of it. Too much to carry.

I spent the next couple days fishing the Green River and picking him up at the end of day. Every evening, I got stories of some of the people he met along the way. They would stop and ask him if he needed a ride. Upon hearing about his venture, they would offer whatever they had on hand in their car.

Dropping Tommy off for the last time was hard. I was eight hours from my family and my bed, but Tommy was looking at another two thousand miles, still traveling light and living without things that frankly, I couldn't live without.

It was a great day when we met in Wyoming, but it was a greater day when I got news that he had made all the way home to New York.

Be like Tommy, the maniac who walked across the country with next to nothing.

AMANDA

I heard about VetZero through Facebook. It may have been one of those things that Facebook recommends following based on your online behavior. (Yikes!) Facebook was part of my job as the Communications Administrator for the City of Green River, so I spent a lot of time scrolling and posting. I clicked for a closer look and saw that this guy, obviously a little nuts or a big fan of Forrest Gump, was trekking across the US and wasn't too far from my little Wyoming town.

I messaged Tommy to see if he planned to come through Green River. I believe he was near Bear Lake which was a few days walk.

As I looked further into Tommy's mission, I hoped he would make it this way. Not only did I want to meet this slightly insane and determined guy, but I also wanted to connect him to the vets in my town. I made a few calls to our American Legion and they were excited to meet him, too.

When Tommy made it to Green River we had a great visit with him. It was so interesting to hear how VetZero worked, how much coordination and sheer faith it took for him to navigate on foot, and how quickly he went through shoes. Of course, I brought my Dad, a vet, with me and Tommy made fast friends with the locals at the Legion. I think he ended up with some donation checks for VetZero, which is certainly the point – raising awareness and funds to help veterans in need.

We made sure he had directions for a walkable path to the next few towns. That's a small-town tribal knowledge kind of thing. That's what I mean by faith; he had to trust the path would be provided when Google Maps failed him. Amazing. We warned him about bears (because Wyoming), took some pics, and gave some hugs.

I was pleased to follow along on Facebook as Tommy made the rest of his journey, re-sharing his posts and cheering him on. I can only imagine the sunrises, mountains, and roadkill he saw along the way.

Glad to know you, Tommy. Thank you for your service, and your continued service of a different kind.

JAMES

I learned about Tommy's VetZero trek from a mutual shipmate of ours, Shayne. I remember seeing a Facebook post Shayne had made about a former shipmate of his walking across the country to raise awareness for veteran suicide. At that point I started following the VetZero updates.

I sent Shayne a message because I saw Tommy's planned trek across Wyoming, and as near as I could tell from his planned map, it looked like he was planning on going from Kemmerer to Jefferey City -- between the two, there is absolutely nothing. So I got concerned and sent Shayne a message to let Tommy know that would be a rough stretch. Even if he stuck to the highways he could get stuck in some terrible weather. I asked Shayne to have Tommy call me because it was looking like it was going to be one of those cold and snowy springs in Wyoming.

Shayne passed on my contact info to Tommy, and thankfully I think he changed his route on his own accord, after seeing what he was up against. Tommy call me on June 3rd and I was glad to hear he had moved the route south and was now following I-80 in southern Wyoming. I believe he arrived in Rawlins on June 4th. I remember I sent a message to the local radio station (bigfoot99) to let them know he was coming and they interviewed him. It was cool to see he came into Rawlins with a little celebrity status.

Tommy and I had dinner at Bucks Sports Grill in Rawlins and I had a chance to learn more about him. He seemed to be incredibly committed to the cause and he definitely left an impression on me. I'm not very good at great descriptive words that describe a man's character but I can say that he is a "Very good dude" and that's about as good as it gets from me.

I run a maintenance crew at a hydro-electric plant and have several veterans on staff so we kept an eye on him as he trekked through our area. We made sure he had coffee and McDonalds Sausage egg muffins every morning. I also ran a rescue mission for his walking stick which got left at a motel in Rawlins. (Thankfully they still had it and I was able to get it to him.) I also got word to veterans in Casper and I think some of them reached out with offers of assistance as well so I knew we would get him the rest of the way across Wyoming safely.

TIM

One day last summer, I was the designated driver going to Lake Alcova with a couple of buddies. They drank and we swam, enjoying a hot day at the beach. All of a sudden, I noticed a man walking toward us and he looked dehydrated. He said that he needed water, and I immediately offered him to drink the melted ice from our cooler. Instead, he asked if we could drive to get him some bottled water, and I remembered a store we passed along the way. So, I drove to the store and bought 3 large bottles of cold water for Tommy. At the time it was no big deal. But I had no idea that small gesture was going to be as meaningful to me as it is today.

I was a homeless Veteran between 2015 and 2018 and Tommy told me he was VetZero, marching across the country to raise awareness for Veteran homelessness. I had been so harmed by PTSD that I couldn't hold a job and had to sign over the rights to my daughter Angela, to prevent going to jail for child support non-payment. I lost everything, slept in shelters, sometimes in hospitals, and usually on the street. The stories I could tell are endless, but I found hope at the Crawford House in Colorado Springs, and ate at a Catholic soup kitchen close by. Then I was sent to Sheridan, Wyoming and fell in love with the state, so being without a car, I moved to the one city in Wyoming with a bus system.

I'm glad Tommy's mission wasn't cut short by means of dehydration that day, and when I got back home I immediately got online to see what his journey was all about. I donated, and got 300+ likes on our photo together. I followed his posts until the end of his journey when he returned home. To this day, it brings me great joy to be part of Tommy's story!

T.C.

I noticed the smell right away. A little like the woods, a little like trash, it's the smell you know from walking very close to homeless people. That was Tommy – or Tellis, to me -- after many, many days of walking along the road and sleeping outside without a shower.

After hearing about Tellis' trip through social media (thanks to my wife) I couldn't stop thinking about what an enormous undertaking the walk was, and my relative ignorance about the cause of veteran suicide and homelessness. I'd been through boot camp with Tellis in 1991 and we've stayed in touch after the Navy. My business has always taken me to New York occasionally and we always manage to catch up in person every few years. I was closely following the walk during the month of May and finally decided I had to do more than simply watch and make a donation. So I made arrangements to get away for a weekend in between a trip to Boston and New York the week of June 3 and a company off-site planned the following week. That meant flying from Toronto, through Denver and into Casper, WY midday Friday, June 7.

I made sure to rent a large SUV, and set off to find Tellis on the road. We'd been in touch via text during the preceding days so I had a general sense of the roads he'd be on and the direction he was heading. After getting off a four-lane highway, then onto a small two-lane road, then finally a dirt road, a few hours later there was the "big guy in the funny hat" making his way along the shoulder of the road. Finally, there he was right in front of me. I pulled over and walked quickly towards, him, we are two big guys so we made a big bear hug right in the middle of the road.

We walked a long way together on our first full day in Casper, along the road for a few hours, then moved onto a trail running parallel to the North Platte River. We ran into a local runner by the veterans' memorial who stopped and realized who Tellis was due to some local radio and TV coverage. Seeing this runner in the middle of nowhere just stop on the trail and ask "are you the guy?"....to which Tellis, unfazed, responded, "yes, I'm Tommy, walking across the country for veteran homelessness" was surreal. We chatted for a few minutes and he took off again like a rabbit. We plodded slowly along. There was a lot of time for us to catch up on our families, and then discussion turned to homelessness in general, and veteran's challenges in particular. I was learning from Tommy, who'd met a lot of people that had been impacted, and had a lot of time to think about it. I remember it dawning on me that a lot of people working hard and living paycheck to paycheck are only one illness or one car repair away from losing their job or transportation, and then missing rent and getting kicked into the street. From there it must be very hard to find another job, make ends meet, and get the chance to get back on your feet. Vets specifically find it hard to ask for help, and thus must really struggle to take advantage of transition programs and the resources made available for civilian transition. There's a mental health issue that also must be dealt with, but that's not something that gets nearly enough attention.

The first thing Tellis wanted to do when we got the outskirts of town was find a coffee shop. After ordering a large cup and downloading messages, a reporter from the local radio station came by (prearranged as we walked into town) for an interview. The local crisis center was generous enough to donate a hotel room for the night, so we found the hotel and got him checked in. The folks from the crisis center also invited the two of us to dinner that night, where we enjoyed a fantastic home cooked meal in the hills surrounding Casper. One of the guests at dinner, the son-in-law of our host, had us all in tears with the story of his best friend from the service, and his tragic death while they served together. He pointed to a metal bracelet around his wrist that he had worn since his friend's death, and not taken off even during a hospital procedure years earlier. He then removed the bracelet, and asked if Tellis would wear it for the rest of his journey, to be reclaimed at the finish. Tellis of course accepted and we were all moved, without a dry eye in the house.

After another day of walking and talking, Tellis and I were on the outskirts of Casper, and it was time for me to get back to the airport and fly home, back to my family and job. I'll never forget the time on the road, the discussions, or how much Tellis' trip has meant to so many.

KEVIN & BERNICE

The stars seemed to align in an uncanny way last summer. Bernice and I had relocated to Casper, Wyoming the previous October. I accepted a position as CEO of Central Wyoming Counseling Center (CWCC) and Bernice, having recently left her position in suicide prevention, was advocating for Wyoming's very first Suicide Prevention Lifeline here at CWCC. Out of the blue we learned from a friend of Bernice's that a Veteran was planning to walk across the country to raise awareness and funds for suicide prevention and he was making a stop in Casper, Wyoming, of all places! Furthermore, he was from Poughkeepsie, our hometown and he was a professor at Marist College which was across the street from where Bernice and I had worked!

We connected with Tommy and we were so pleased that we were able to meet him on his incredible journey. Knowing how harsh and unforgiving the weather can be in this part of the country we expected him to be exhausted. He had to contend with some snow and unrelenting wind. He arrived here on June 8th and we had the pleasure of sharing several meals with him and one of his Veteran buddies. Tommy had managed to keep his positive attitude and we were able to arrange for him to meet some local veterans who shared some of their experiences with him. Tommy's journey was truly inspirational and we enjoyed following his exploits as he completed his epic walk. Bernice especially looked forward to hearing his interpretation of popular songs that he provided while he walked. By the way, Bernice succeeded in starting up the lifeline, she is Director of the National Suicide Prevention Lifeline at CWCC!!

RICH

During the summer of 2019, my son asked me to help out a friend of his. It seemed a guy he knew from the University of Alabama was walking across America, to draw attention to the problems of our military veterans. And, since he was soon to be in our part of the world in Iowa, could I help him for a few days with whatever he needed?

I readily agreed.

Over the next few days we went from what I thought would be a causal acquaintance to what is now shaping up to be a lifetime friendship! Our entire family, as well as several members of the community, loved our visit from Tommy, as we wished him well and helped him with his cause.

On the last day of our visit, I dropped Tommy off in Twin Lakes, Iowa. As I helped him out of the van, I had a feeling of loneliness come over me, and I asked, "Tommy, are you going to be all right?" He assured me he would.

"But," I added, "you don't know anybody here."

He smiled. "Not yet."

I drove up the street two blocks and came back for a final drive-by. There was Tommy, already talking to three people and everybody was smiling. I waved good-bye to my friend Tommy, the walking sailor.

JANANN

I knew Tommy as a kid – we were campers together. He was one of those people who knew everyone's name, always had a smile and a story, and everyone liked him. I have to admit, we were not close friends, but friendships built in summer camp are unique and life-long. Eventually I lost touch with Tommy, but social media and camp reunions have rectified that situation in more recent years. When I heard about VetZero, I knew I wanted to help. Well, first I thought he was out of his mind, and then I knew I wanted support the effort!

When we pulled up at a park outside of Dodge City, Iowa, there was Tommy, lying flat on his back in the grass. He looked sunburnt and tired, but otherwise he was the same spirit I knew all those years ago – prepared with a smile and story to greet us! Over dinner, the stories continued and I was mesmerized. Tommy had met so many wonderful people along the way, and carried bits of them with him – from a handmade walking stick to the stories of both hard times and victories of individuals who had served our country. It wasn't until spending the night in Fort Dodge when I started to really understand the people and efforts we were supporting – I had driven north to Iowa to support an old friend, but we left Iowa with a whole new understanding and appreciation for veterans everywhere. Honestly, I cannot look at our flag, talk to veterans, or think about foot travel without realizing how indebted we are to those who have served, and all the ways we need to return that support and respect to those who have done so much. And woven throughout all those thoughts is Tommy's smile and warmth.

Thank you, Tommy, my old friend!

RICHARD

I first learned of Tommy's cross-country adventure through a local charity here in southern Wisconsin called *VetsRoll*, and that's when I started to follow his progress on social media. As a veteran myself I thought, "What a bold and noble cause," and immediately started sharing his travels with family, friends, and veteran groups I'm involved with. As I followed his progress step after step, song after song, city after city and learned he was coming through my old hometown of Beloit, Wisconsin I knew I had to meet the "big man in the funny hat" and there was a no more fitting place to do it than Beloit College. You see, when I was first discharged from the Navy the college took a chance on this "Townie" (as the kids called us) and hired me as the manager of their on campus watering hole, The Coffee Haus. As I watched Tommy doing his live videos and getting the word out about veteran homelessness I noticed he had this little walking stick he was using, and I thought to myself, he could use something with some backbone.

So off to the woodshop I went. I knew I needed to come up with something that would represent VetZero and the message Tommy was spreading throughout our country on his journey. I thought, what could be more fitting than the good ole Red, White and Blue? It was my honor to make his walking stick, and even more of an honor to meet a fellow Brother in Arms on his mission to walk across America.

DAVE

My wife, Donna, and I own Naked Dove Brewing Company in Canandaigua, NY. My connection with Tommy and his cross-coun-try walk started, as many things do these days, through a Facebook post. My old friend from college, Paul, went to Nuclear Power School in the Navy with Tommy and last April, Paul posted about

Tommy's journey on Facebook. Intrigued, I followed the link to VetZero and saw that Tommy's schedule would bring him through Canandaigua in August. It appeared to be fate, so I reached out to Paul to see how we could get involved.

Fast forward four months (and 2000+ miles for Tommy) to August. Through Paul, I contacted Tommy and coordinated a Happy Hour at Naked Dove with all the pint sales going to VetZero. Tommy would end his walk here that day and meet with our customers so that we could raise some money for the cause. Paul, who had walked the first leg with Tommy, decided to fly out from Portland and come to the Happy Hour and walk another leg of the journey with Tommy.

There are so many memorable parts to the day and a half that I spent with Tommy. I was able to hear the stories from the journey (I did not know antelope screamed), catch up with my good friend Paul, who I hadn't seen in 25 years, and witness the generosity of our customers. Out of it all, there were two incidents that will always be part of me. When Tommy arrived, even though you could tell he was exhausted, he worked the room like a pro. There was a local newspaper reporter to whom he gave an interview and he talked to all the people who had come out to support him that evening. Waiting very patiently to talk to Tommy, but with a lot of pride and excitement, was the son of a couple who are regulars. He is about 10 years old and his parents had explained to him what Tommy was doing and why it was important. The boy decided to make Tommy a gift. When it was their turn, the boy presented Tommy with a small rock that had the American flag painted on it with the words 'Thank You' written underneath. The boy was excited and proud but a little apprehensive to present it to Tommy. Tommy was visibly moved by the gift and was able to make the boy feel at ease. It was a beautiful to witness someone so young get involved in the only way he knew how.

The second moment was very personal for Tommy. There was

a young woman who came in and ordered a pint. I served her the pint and as she waited for Tommy, I saw her drop a $50 bill in the donation basket. When Tommy saw her, you could tell he was genuinely excited. It turned out she was a student of his who had graduated that year and was living in Rochester. He was thrilled that she came out and talked to her for a while. At the end of the night, after everyone had left Tommy, Paul and I were talking while having one last beer at the brewery. He mentioned how happy he was that his student had come in to see him, how special it was to him. At this point, I told Tommy about her generosity; he was moved to tears. His first concern was for her. She had recently graduated and did not have the sort of money to be that generous. Paul and I reinforced to Tommy the true effect that he was having on people. Not only the Veterans who were going to benefit from the money and awareness that was raised but also the enlightenment that he was providing to the rest of us. His student and her generosity were emblematic of this fact.

At the end of the night, our event had raised $1000 for VetZero at the Happy Hour and another $450 from Naked Dove customers who could not make it but donated through Go Fund Me. Tommy and Paul crashed at my house and walked the next leg together the following day. I am extremely proud that I was able to contribute to the success of Tommy's journey. I am proud of the Naked Dove Family that we have created and their generosity. It was a whirlwind, but it was a great couple of days. It reminded me of why we work so hard to create the type of business where our customers are family, and are supportive of the things we believe in. That is truly what life is all about.

RYAN

When Tommy first announced his mission to walk across the country, I knew right then and there I'd have to follow his journey, from start to finish. His dedication to raising awareness on the grim realities of veteran suicide and veteran homelessness resonated with me, as I am a veteran myself. What he set out to do, and achieved, is nothing short of admirable. Seeing the local community as well as people all around the country come together and donate to his cause was something very special to not only witness, but to partake in as well.

Luckily enough for me, being a Security Officer at Marist College, I was also able to participate in the last day of his walk, providing personal security for his route from New Paltz to the Marist College campus. Starting in the early morning and officially meeting Tommy for the first time, it was hard not to feel a little "star struck" for having the opportunity to take part in something special with this local legend! We walked thirteen miles that day talking, laughing, and sweating our way back to campus. Being greeted on the Walkway over the Hudson by local government officials and an abundance of local supporters was an incredible thing to experience. Route 9 being shut down and bagpipers escorting us to the main gates of campus was very surreal for me, and I can only imagine how it felt for him. Tommy was an absolute celebrity in this moment, and I was proud to be there alongside him.

After thirteen miles I felt pretty beat up, but proud to have finished alongside him. The soreness my body felt after thirteen miles made me recognize the weight that Tommy must have carried by walking almost TWENTY-TWO MILES a day! Unbelievable. Furthermore, that made me think of the unseen, unknown homeless veterans who carry this weight every day because unfortunately, that's their reality. What Tommy did and continues to do in our community, is truly a beautiful thing.

As a member of the Red Fox community, as a United States Army Veteran, and as a human, I am proud to have the absolute pleasure and honor of sharing a small portion of this journey with him.

JULIA

I was excited about the VetZero project from the beginning. But I'm also a realist. I Googled people who had walked/biked/run across the country for different issues and there were plenty of examples. So, although I really believed in Tommy's project, I understood that the physical endeavor wasn't groundbreaking. I also understood that if he was injured in Oregon, there would be no story to tell.

My strategy was to hold a kick-off press conference on the Marist campus for Tommy in April, before he flew out west. It went well with all major regional media attending. After that, I pitched market by market based on Tommy's route. No outlet was too small—I sent press advisories to everyone and did follow-up. I got coverage in every state, but it was Iowa where things picked up and then I got Tommy an in-studio interview with a morning new program in Milwaukee. That changed everything. I was pitching the major networks in New York, saying he had walked over 1,000 miles. While doing research for a feel-good, human-interest story, a producer at *NBC Nightly News* saw the Milwaukee interview and then we were really flying.

The night before the final day of the walk, I actually saw Tommy at the Mansion, where he was spending the night before the final leg. Right before I left my office to drive there, I felt really emotional and was teary; although I wasn't the one doing the walking, in some ways it felt like it was my journey, too.

After almost five months, the final day arrived. Ironically, I was meeting Tommy and the *NBC Nightly News* crew on my home turf in New Paltz. The producer had hit some traffic and was late, and Tommy was understandably getting nervous about staying on schedule. The producer, of course, had some specific shots in mind she wanted and being a public relations professional, I wanted to oblige. But knowing Tommy fairly well, I could also sense his stress, so I was trying to keep the process moving. The camera crew thought they could drive slowly down New Paltz's Main Street getting Tommy as he walked. It's a small town, but traffic can be heavy and I assured him people would not be kind toward that behavior on a one-lane road. The cameraman rode in the open back of an SUV, legs dangling, holding a very expensive camera. I was worried about Tommy's stress level, but was also kind of freaked out about the cameraman falling out of the vehicle and getting hurt.

Luckily that didn't happen.

They got the shots they wanted and I'll never forget Tommy saying to me, "I want to get out of here." So I spoke to the producer and her crew and told them plainly, Tommy needed to get moving. The rest of the day was a blur after that. The rest of the day was a blur: phone calls, emails, texts, coordinating with regional media, getting to campus for the return celebration. I came home that night and collapsed on my sofa. The next thing I really remember was watching *NBC Nightly News* that Sunday, hoping our segment would air — when it finally did, I felt I could breathe again.

JOHNNY Z.

It hit me on the bridge. The world's longest elevated pedestrian bridge, to be exact. "The Walkway over the Hudson." The bridge marked the final miles of my brother's trek across America. That morning, my brother had three walking companions. Now, halfway across the bridge, he's got over a thousand. Close friends and complete strangers, news reporters and politicians, all trying to keep pace with the man. But the man doesn't stop. He won't sign autographs, he won't kiss babies. He's not doing anything but putting one foot in front of the other. Walking. What he's been doing every day for the last five months. I try to keep pace, too, alongside the hundreds of cheering, clapping, laughing supporters.

Everyone's feeling a foot taller, throwing their shoulders back with pride, the hot August sun warming their faces. Kids try to run ahead and turn around quickly enough to snap a picture of the man, but he still doesn't stop. He's walking. It's like something out of a Rocky movie, although no movie studio could afford this many extras.

Then, it hit me: this movie is so much better than Rocky. And it stars my big brother, Tommy. The crowds squeeze against me. They all want to get closer to him. I fade back, letting them pour past me. I watch my brother get farther away, exit the bridge and hit the streets of Poughkeepsie. Firefighters with fire engines block traffic as the hundreds of supporters become thousands.

One man can make a difference.

Tommy's that man. And he always will be, to me.

CHRISTA

I remember clearly getting the email from the new Commander of the local VFW, Tommy Zurhellen. I've been the Executive Director of Hudson River Housing for a long time, and we are very fortunate to have all sorts of people reach out to us, trying to find out how they can help us with our mission of serving the homeless, especially serving veterans who are homeless. Never did I think for a minute, though, that this simple email would lead to a friendship and partnership like I have with Tommy. Just a few days after I got the email, I was sitting across the table in my office from the formidable and ambitious Commander – as advertised, he's a very big guy – and we were already developing countless strategies to eradicate homelessness, fix all that was wrong in our community, and take on the world, just for starters! Although I have had plenty of similar conversations with well-minded and driven people, there was something different about Tommy. I knew he was going to make a difference – not sure exactly how – but I knew it. And I was right!

A few months later, we were having a beer at our favorite, after-work spot, and he starts telling me how he's turning 50 soon, and has some big plans. I took a deep breath and listened, not really sure what was coming next, although knowing Tommy, I knew it was probably going to be something pretty big. Well, we all know what he told me – that he was going to walk across the country to raise awareness and funds for our cause – and that he was flying out to Portland, Oregon in April with only a backpack and some water and a new pair of sneakers on his feet.

We all now know the outcome of Tommy's incredible journey. But you know what? I am still simply in awe of his commitment and dedication to doing what he believes in – no fear, just faith. It is my truest pleasure and honor to call him my friend and I am so grateful to know him. He has inspired me beyond measure and I can't wait to be a part of what he thinks up next! There is no stopping the 'big guy with the funny hat' and I thank God for that.

DR. DENNIS MURRAY
PRESIDENT OF MARIST COLLEGE

I've always believed that a nation owes its military veterans a great debt. It's not only the right thing to do, it's also in the country's best interest. George Washington understood this and had the following advice: "The willingness with which our young people are likely to serve in any war, no matter how justified, shall be directly proportional to how the veterans of earlier wars were treated and appreciated by their nation." Tommy Zurhellen helped our nation live up to this principle, as well as the principle of service, which is so central to the ethos of Marist College. In fact, Tommy's extraordinary trek across the United States stands as the most powerful example of service I've ever seen. Over the course of four months, he walked 2,860 miles across eight states for one simple yet compelling reason: he saw a chance to help veterans in need, and he was prepared to go the distance.

From April to August 2019 – day in and day out – Tommy covered 22 miles a day to honor the 22 veterans who take their own lives on an average day in America. Countless other veterans in our country struggle with homelessness, substance abuse, and mental illness. It's a national tragedy demanding a response, and Tommy decided to give it the attention it deserves. He put his entire life on hold and showed how one person can have a significant positive impact and inspire others.

It's hard to wrap your mind around the mechanics of walking 22 miles each and every day, no matter the weather or how tired and sore you are. How did Tommy find the strength to keep going? What propelled him forward? As he himself will tell you, it's because he realized that his pain paled in comparison to that of his fellow veterans. That deep desire to serve others in need was what pushed Tommy to continue on, day after day and mile after mile.

And Tommy's commitment to service did inspire others. He blew through his fundraising goal of $40,387 (a figure representing the average number of homeless veterans on a given day in America) and far surpassed it. Donations poured in from supporters all along his route, and our local charities supporting veterans received a major boost as a result. Thanks to extensive media coverage, the story of Tommy's journey reached an estimated 152 million people. If just a fraction of those people who heard about his walk were inspired to be of service in their own communities, the contribution to the greater good would be incalculable.

Tommy returned to the Marist campus on August 23, 2019, and it was one of the proudest days of my life. As he passed through our main gates, he was welcomed not only by members of the Marist community, but also by a large crowd of grateful veterans, ROTC cadets, elected officials, members of law enforcement, and community leaders. I believe that everyone in attendance that day was moved by Tommy's selflessness and dedication to a cause larger than himself. What he really demonstrated was the power of one individual to change the world, or at least their part of the world. Tommy's project serves as an open invitation to us all to put service at the center of our lives. In putting it at the center of his life, he has exemplified not only the best values of our nation, but also the best values of Marist College.

PHOTOGRAPHS

This is it! The first selfie, right before Paul and I take the very first steps of the walk in Portland. Such optimistic faces!

So much for optimism. Ouch.

My old shipmates Jeff and Shayne and others walked a leg with me through their hometown of Boise, Idaho. Get some!

"I turned around in traffic just to meet you," Bob said in Burley, Idaho. "I hope it's worth it." (Me too, Bob.)

The Bear Lake's Sheriff's Department rescued me with some warm gear on a cold, windy day in northeast Utah.

In Casper, Wyoming, Masa asked me to wear this bracelet the rest of the way, to remember his fallen battle buddy Ricky.

Back at the Poughkeepsie VFW, Bethann provided the "nonline" version of Facebook for folks to keep up on my progress.

Hands down, my favorite part of the journey was meeting veterans all across America, like these heroes in Correctionville, Iowa.

After the mountains of Wyoming, the flat cornfields of the Midwest felt like a vacation. Closing in on Iowa here.

Being able to help veterans in Flint, Michigan, was a very special honor for me. It turned out to be special for Christa, as well.

Paul returned long enough for us to visit his buddy Dave at Naked Dove Brewing for an awesome VetZero fundraiser.

My phone kept track of my steps &
mileage. This day must have been very
flat, since that step count is low for 23
miles.

Mickey and Bert leading the way on Day 130, right before we got soaked
by a downpour of Biblical proportions.

Christa and I were overwhelmed by the crowd waiting for us on the Marist campus at the end of the VetZero Walk Across America

ACKNOWLEDGMENTS

To all the veterans across America who are struggling, this book is dedicated to you.

Harry Truman once said, "It's amazing what you can accomplish, when you don't care who gets the credit." That certainly sounds great on paper, but in reality, it's a hard lesson to grasp in the ultra-competitive, conflicted world we find ourselves in today. Thankfully, over the past year I've had two opportunities to learn that important lesson: first, by walking across America, and second, by trying to write about it.

Both times, it was a valuable lesson in humility.

Sure, I walked across America alone, but I could never have done it on my own. There are so many folks who deserve credit for the walk, and the completion of this book you're holding in your hands right now. I can't possibly thank them all for their incredible kindness, grace and hospitality. Some people I met on the road – everyone from the two guys who ran out from their warehouse to bring me water in Nebraska, to the young female Army veteran I spoke with at a gas station in Wisconsin – wished to remain anonymous, and I respect that. So to everyone who helped me get where I was going during the summer of 2019, please accept my heartfelt thanks. Please know that every time I take a long walk, I automatically think of our encounters on the low road.

Thanks to the team at Marist College, especially Nora and Julia, who managed to share the VetZero story with over twelve million Americans. Thanks to Carlo for those great photographs, and thanks to Coach Pete for all the advice and chutzpah along the way. Thanks also to my Marist colleagues Amy, Em, Geoff, Chris, Elisabeth, Tim, and the Colonel for lending your talents and resources to support the project. Thanks to Colin for the good luck charm, and thanks to all my students for your enthusiasm. And of course, thank you to President Dennis Murray, for allowing his faculty to carry out the Marist tradition of engaging in the social good, even when the plan sounds a little bizarre. I will never forget that magical last day of the walk.

Thanks to my "Gang of Six" comrades at VFW Post 170 who truly supported this adventure and embraced the hard work of community service, while many others at our Post did not. Special thanks to Bethann for all your work putting together the "non-line" version of our social media posts, so everyone at the VFW could follow the journey.

Thanks to all the friends, new and old, who joined me on the trail, shined a light, and helped me find the way home. I couldn't have made it without you. Thanks to Mark, Josiah, Carl, Janann, Kevin, Bernice, Baker, Amanda, Rich, Danielle aka Sugar, Susan, Karen at Beloit College, Uncle Robert, and Dave at Naked Dove Brewing for various rescues on the road. Thanks to my fabulous cousins for walking a day with me in Detroit. Thanks to Brian in Flint for putting together a wonderful event on short notice. Thanks to my best friend Jeff for the jump-off, and to Doris for bringing me home.

Thanks to the hundreds of veterans I met while walking the low road, like Topher, Bob, Windhorse, Rusty, and so many others.

Your stories will always hold the highest place in my heart. Special thanks to my old shipmates Paul, Jeff, Shayne, and T.C. for coming out and helping to carry the weight. Thanks to Masa, for allowing me to walk with Ricky, and thanks to my new shipmate Richard in Beloit, for the amazing walking stick.

Thanks to Lester Holt and his team at *NBC Nightly News* for taking a chance on a big guy in a funny hat, and thanks to Molly and the *Morning Blend* in Milwaukee for giving us our first big break. Thanks to my friends Boris and Robyn at WPDH, and thanks to the dozens of local news outfits who picked up our story along the way, especially my stellar former student Bern for her brilliant feature in the *New York Post*. Thanks to my writing mentor Michael Martone for reading early drafts of this book, and of course, for the winnowing oar. Thanks also to Epigraph Press for crafting this exclusive VetZero Heroes Edition of *The Low Road* to benefit veterans in the Hudson Valley.

Perennial bouquets of thanks to my trusted editor and longtime friend Virginia Konchan, for taking great care with this book. *Encore une fois, tu as transformé mes balles en papillons!*

Finally, thank you to my friend Christa. You were the only person who believed in me from the very start of this bizarre adventure. Thanks for being my Sancho Panza on this Quest for the Holy Fail; I'm already looking forward to returning the favor, when we concoct our next plan to make the world a better place.

REQUIRED READING

At Marist, we try to teach our students that good writers must be good readers, too. Lord, I hope that's true, because I've pored through a busload of books looking for inspiration as I wrote *The Low Road* over the past year. (Thank goodness no one ever says, *good writers must be good dancers*, because then I would be in serious trouble.) If you are thinking about creating your own fool-hardy adventure to stoke your own passions and make a difference in the world, I suggest starting at the library. Here's an eclectic reading list about walking, writing, and altruism that inspired and educated me; I hope they spark something for you, too.

Wild: From Lost to Found on the Pacific Coast Trail by Cheryl Strayed
Walking the Amazon by Ed Stafford
A Walk in the Woods by Bill Bryson
Tracks by Robyn Davidson
Travels with Charley by John Steinbeck
A Walk Across America by Peter Jenkins
Off the Road by Jack Hitt
A Man in a Hurry by Nick Harris
Rising Strong by Brené Brown
The Most Good You Can Do by Peter Singer

The Low Road

Enrique's Journey by Sonia Nazario
Into Thin Air by Jon Krakauer
Lit by Mary Karr
Brooding by Michael Martone

ABOUT THIS EDITION

All net proceeds from this special **VetZero Heroes Edition** of *The Low Road* will go directly to helping veterans in need. VetZero is proud to partner with Hudson River Housing in Poughkeepsie, New York. Thank you so much for your support!

We envision a world where no one is homeless, and where everyone has the opportunity to live in safe, affordable, and appropriate housing where they can thrive, regardless of income, family makeup, physical or mental health issues, or any other defining factors. We envision a world where there is sufficient housing available for all, and where communities, including their residents and governing bodies, understand and value safe, affordable, and well-designed housing and neighborhoods as essential to everyday life and well-being.

To find out more about Hudson River Housing and its mission, visit their website:

www.hudsonriverhousing.org

ABOUT THE AUTHOR

Tommy Zurhellen is the author of the award-winning Messiah Trilogy of novels, which reimagine the life of Jesus in rural America: *Nazareth, North Dakota* (2011), *Apostle Islands* (2012) and *Armageddon, Texas* (2014), all from Atticus Books. His short stories have appeared widely, in *Carolina Quarterly*, *Passages North*, *Quarterly West*, *Crab Creek Review* and elsewhere. His popular column on veterans' issues "Dispatches from the VFW" appears regularly in the Dutchess Newspapers, and he still appears weekly on the Boris & Robyn Show on WPDH 101.5FM in the Hudson Valley to deliver a veterans' update. He served honorably in the United States Navy as a Nuclear Electrician onboard the USS Truxtun and USS California. With the help of the G.I. Bill, he received his M.F.A. in Fiction from the University of Alabama, and now teaches Creative Writing at Marist College, which is regularly celebrated as a "Best Regional University" and a "Best College for Veterans" by *U.S. News & World Report*. This is his first memoir.

CPSIA information can be obtained
at www.ICGtesting.com
Printed in the USA
FSHW011127160521